Praise for *The Kindness Advantage*

"In this day and age, kindness and connection are especially important. An accessible and informative guide, *The Kindness Advantage* is a must-read for parents of all ages."

—**Judson Brewer MD, PhD,** Author of *The Craving Mind: From Cigarettes to Smartphones to Love—Why We Get Hooked and How We Can Break Bad Habits*

"*The Kindness Advantage* is the perfect book. Building on scientific evidence about developing aspects of kindness, such as empathy, it gives clear, practical advice to parents and suggests engaging activities and stories for children. Nothing could be more important today than increasing compassion and decreasing polarization and acrimony. I am going to give this book to my son who has a young daughter."

—**Susan Fuhrman, PhD,** President Emerita, Teachers College Columbia University

"In times of discord and polarization, kindness is a family value that can often be overlooked and underestimated. But, in truth, few parental responsibilities carry more weight—and bring more joy—than teaching children the power of flexing their own kindness muscles. Steeped in research and brimming with practical tips, *The Kindness Advantage* provides parents with a blueprint for nurturing empathy in young children, while offering real-life stories that both instruct and inspire. This is a thoughtful guidebook for parents, caregivers, and any adults looking to help build happiness, raise good citizens, and create harmonious communities."

—**Myung Lee,** Executive Director of Fund for Cities of Service

"*The Kindness Advantage* by Dale Atkins, PhD, and Amanda Salzhauer, MSW, is exactly what we need more of right now. With empowering examples and science-based truths, Dale and Amanda share what it takes to foster kindness, empathy, compassion, and heart in our families. Parents will learn how to take on social questions and connect in a way that will improve the lives of their children and help create a more nurturing world. Highly recommended!"

—**Amy McCready,** Author and Founder, Positive Parenting Solutions

"As a physician who uses mindfulness practices extensively in working with patients, health care professionals, and people dealing with all varieties of stress, I love that this book incorporates those practices into a guide for parents who are teaching their children to be kind. The authors wisely lead with the evidence that kindness leads to greater happiness, meaning, and wellbeing, and then provide a myriad of inspirational examples and ideas for children and parents. Grandparents, who are often crucial inspirational figures in children's lives, may particularly benefit from ideas for intergenerational collaborations in kindness."

—Patricia A. Bloom, MD
Certified Teacher of Mindfulness-Based Stress Reduction
Clinical Associate Professor of Geriatrics, Mount Sinai Medical Center

"Just like we see in kids who have the empathy advantage, children who are raised with the kindness advantage are happier, connected, compassionate, and will have what they need to become change-makers in their world. *The Kindness Advantage* offers parents the tools to teach these skills and more to their young children. With the extensive examples of activities provided in the *The Kindness Advantage*, parents can pick and choose what resonates with them to create a personalized approach to bringing kindness into their everyday lives."

—Michele Borba, EdD, Author of *UnSelfie: Why Empathetic Kids Succeed in Our All-About-Me World*

"*The Kindness Advantage* is the ray of hope that we all need in this harsh, heavy, world. It is a blueprint of how to partner with the next generation to live our inherent values, to tap our organic ability to love, and to create a kinder culture. Many thanks to Dale Atkins and Amanda Salzhauer for bringing this much-needed gift to the world!"

—Rev. Susan Sparks,
Pastor, Comedian, and Author of *Laugh Your Way to Grace*

"Dale Atkins and Amanda Salzhauer's book, *The Kindness Advantage*, can serve as a partial antidote to these turbulent times. They remind us that kindness is both a moral behavior that can improve the status of the world, but also be advantageous to the individual who practices kindness. The book's blend of significant and relevant issues in psychology, education, and humanism provides a myriad of practical suggestions to help us raise kind children. The book will serve as a resource to parents and educators. By teaching the components underlying kindness children can be provided a framework where we can both teach and weave these crucial lessons into the lives of children.

The section on relaxation, breathing, visualization and mediation is a gift to the children in our lives and ourselves. We cannot impart the lessons of kindness when we ourselves are agitated and distressed by the tumult in our lives and in our worlds. Likewise, children have difficulty being kind when they are in the grip of negative emotions. This section provides children and adults the tools to master negative emotions. We highly recommend this book to be read, saved and used as a long term resource in your child-rearing library."

—**Norma D. Feshbach, PhD**, Professor, Chair, Interim Dean Emeritus UCLA and
Laura E. Feshbach, PhD

"With optimism and compassion, *The Kindness Advantage* offers practical tips and real-world examples parents and educators need to teach empathy, compassion, and kindness to our children. Along the way, it also provides opportunities to reflect on our values and experiences as adults. This book speaks to the innate desire of every child to be good to themselves and those around them. Dale Atkins and Amanda Salzhauer make the case for kindness as the tool to radically transform our children's lives, and our own."

—**Naila Bolus**, President and CEO, Jumpstart

"It is through kindness that we find inner peace, and understanding of our humanity, our interconnectedness. Thank you, Dale Atkins and Amanda Salzhauer, for gifting us with *The Kindness Advantage*, a guide to share this most powerful and important tool with our children."

—**Janet Slom, MFA**, Founder, Mindfulness-Based Self Expression

"*The Kindness Advantage* provides practical wisdom and good-sense guidance to help you scaffold your child's journey toward goodness of heart. This book is a gift which has arrived at the perfect time for our world."

—**Amishi Jha, PhD**, Neuroscientist and Researcher

"Before we expect kindness from others, we have to nurture it in ourselves. Thanks to *The Kindness Advantage* we now have the recipe to raise children that better the world not because of what they have done, but because of who they are. And, in the process, we can learn to become kinder people in an often divisive and complicated world."

—**Rabbi Sherre Hirsch**, Author, *We Plan, God Laughs*

The
kindness
ADVANTAGE

CULTIVATING COMPASSIONATE and CONNECTED CHILDREN

EVERYDAY IDEAS FOR RAISING KIDS WHO CARE

Dale Atkins, PhD, and
Amanda Salzhauer, MSW

Health Communications, Inc.
Deerfield Beach, Florida

www.hcibooks.com

Library of Congress Cataloging-in-Publication Data
is available through the Library of Congress

© 2018 Dale Atkins, PhD, and Amanda Salzhauer, MSW

ISBN-13: 978-07573-2099-6 (Paperback)
ISBN-10: 07573-2099-6 (Paperback)
ISBN-13: 978-07573-2100-9 (ePub)
ISBN-10: 07573-2100-3 (ePub)

Publisher: Health Communications, Inc.
       3201 S.W. 15th Street
       Deerfield Beach, FL 33442–8190

Cover and interior design and formatting by Lawna Patterson Oldfield

Contents

ix | Foreword

xi | Preface

1 | Introduction

Part One: Getting Started

7 | Chapter 1: **Why Kindness?**

15 | Chapter 2: **Setting a Positive Example**

Part Two: Take It In

25 | Chapter 3: **The Fundamentals of Kindness**
⟹ Acceptance ⟹ Commitment ⟹ Connection ⟹ Empathy
⟹ Giving ⟹ Interest ⟹ Nurturing ⟹ Observing
⟹ Questioning ⟹ (Be) Yourself

Part Three: Taking It Further

61 | Chapter 4: **Approaching Tough Conversations**

73 | Chapter 5: **Finding Formal Experiences**

85 | Chapter 6: **The Importance of Relaxation: Tools for Breathing, Visualization, and Meditation**

105 | Chapter 7: **Troubleshooting**

119 | Conclusion

121 | **Resources**

   122 Recommended Picture Books

   126 Recommended Reading for Older Kids

   128 Recommended Reading for Adults

   130 Apps, Websites, CDs

   133 Journal Pages

   148 End Notes

   151 Acknowledgments

Foreword

As an educational psychologist with a focus on empathy and char-acter development, I recognize the challenge of raising children who are compassionate and caring. In our uber-technologically connected world, these qualities are often hard to come by. For parents who value them, and want to nurture habits of kindness in their children, the key, as Atkins and Salzhauer emphasize, is starting young.

I have devoted my career to studying the socio-emotional development of children, including the underpinnings of bullying, and how empathy, altruism, and resilience impact our children. I have also explored the fields of social competence, self-esteem, and the prevention of violence. Research in each of these areas illuminates the key role parents play in their children's moral development.

The Kindness Advantage presents current research about kindness and compassion in children. It is filled with real life examples of children who found creative and meaningful ways to connect with others to make a difference in the world. Thoroughly accessible, the authors provide smart, practical suggestions for nurturing young children's innate kindness. Additionally, you will find scripts to teach mindfulness and relaxation to your children. You can call on these scripts to help your child enhance everyday experiences as well as calm anxiety in challenging situations.

Children who are raised with the kindness advantage are happier, more connected, compassionate, and will have what they need to become change makers in their world. That is why the authors' encouragement to nurture a spirit of kindness in the daily life of children is so vital. *The Kindness Advantage* offers parents and grandparents the tools to teach these skills and more to their young children. With the extensive examples of activities provided in the *The Kindness Advantage*, parents can pick and choose what resonates with them to create a personalized approach to bringing kindness into their everyday lives. Kudos to my colleagues for writing the right book for this moment in time.

—**Michele Borba, EdD**, Bestselling Author of
*UnSelfie: Why Empathetic Kids Succeed
in Our All-About-Me World*

Preface

In homes and school communities nationwide, there is re-energized interest in the values of community, compassion, and tolerance, and in finding our way to a kinder culture—a culture that starts with our families. Headlines speak of hate crimes, intolerance, and us-versus-them divisiveness. Recent political events have left many Americans yearning for unity, respect, and compassion in our national discourse. In our schools, bullying continues to be a pervasive problem, and in our homes, "screen time" poses a constant threat to "family time." Research shows that connection and social engagement are key to successful, fulfilling lives, and yet we have never been less connected than we are now. Perhaps more than any other group, parents recognize the potential damage of this trend.

Children who are raised in a culture where giving and compassion are valued become happier and more positively engaged with those around them. They are less likely to treat others disrespectfully. With increased concern about meanness and bullying, you may be among the many parents who see the need for more civil, respectful, and considerate behavior among our children.

Dr. Richard Davidson, renowned psychologist, neuroscientist, and leader in the field of emotion and the brain is founder and chair of the

Center for Healthy Minds at the University of Wisconsin–Madison. He characterized the current situation in this way, "I think that there is a recognition among very large segments of the population that there are better ways of conducting ourselves, and the scientific research that we've been doing can play a small role in helping to catalyze change, in helping to show that things the way they are, are not inevitable…that we can actually take more responsibility of our own minds and transform our minds in ways that will promote increased cooperation, kindness, and increased well-being, and also a greater sensitivity to the environment around us so that we can be better caretakers of the planet. So I think that this is a hopeful sign amid other distressing characteristics, but one that gives me confidence that there is a very bright future for humanity."

Since you have picked up this book, you're like many others who are interested in teaching your child how to make the world a better place. There are countless opportunities but where do you start? How do you figure out what is right for you and your family? In response to a renewed interest in the values of community, compassion, and kindness, we wrote *The Kindness Advantage*. It is based on a simple yet powerful premise: that living a compassionate life, one in which kindness is highly valued, is the key to our children's current and future well-being.

The Kindness Advantage is a practical and concrete guide for you to equip your child with the necessary skills to have a positive influence on the world. This book goes well beyond teaching "please" and "thank-you." It will help your child form compassionate habits that will last a lifetime. We all benefit when children are raised with the understanding that they can have an impact by making conscious choices. It's never too early to start your child on a path of fulfillment through meaningful connection with others.

By way of introduction: We are both mental health professionals who have devoted our lives to working with families and children. We are a mom and grandma. We are an aunt and niece team. We share experiences from our work lives and values from our own family. We originally set out to write a book about raising charitable children. Along the way, we realized that being charitable (which we see as helping others) is not just about charity. We have observed that certain characteristics appear to be an integral part of exceptionally charitable people. We believe that with very few exceptions, each of us is born with these characteristics. We can learn to recognize and pay attention to how we incorporate them into our daily life and nurture them in our children. These concepts are vital to living a caring and purposeful life. We hope *The Kindness Advantage* will help your whole family discover ways to make a positive impact in the world.

*To our families—
with love and gratitude.*

Introduction

Of course you want to help your child make the world a better place; that's why you picked up this book. With meanness and bullying so prevalent, you may be among the many parents desperate to have kids engage in more civil, respectful, and considerate behavior. You may be part of the national conversation about fostering compassion and kindness in children. You may be looking to start with one child—yours.

Research shows that when you talk to your kids about giving to others, and provide them with opportunities to do so, they are more likely to be happy and have a positive influence on the world. In short, "doing good for others benefits the giver." Our original plan was to write a book about *teaching* children how to be compassionate and charitable. But as we interviewed people who are exceptionally charitable, we discovered that most of them shared similar fundamental characteristics. These characteristics—such as acceptance, empathy, and commitment—seemed integral to their very being.

Suddenly, a light bulb went off: rather than teach children *how* to be kind, why not simply nurture those qualities already within them, qualities that lead to compassionate behavior? Studies show that infants between six and ten months old "assess individuals on the basis of their behavior towards others."[1] They show preference for helping over neutral

1

or hindering behaviors. These helping behaviors are what we want to encourage in our children. Observing, questioning, and understanding are characteristics not only essential to being charitable, but vital to living a caring and purposeful life. First, we as parents must recognize them. Next, we find ways to nurture them in our everyday life. Finally, we teach them to our children.

How do we do this? In *The Kindness Advantage*, we help you uncover your child's compassionate qualities. Practical, concrete suggestions will help you and your child practice kindness in everyday life. Understanding these fundamental characteristics will give you the tools to shape and strengthen your child's "kindness" neuropathways. Before you know it, your family will become kindness superheroes!

Each fundamental characteristic includes an introduction for you, along with:

1) Text to be read and discussed with your child
2) Questions to help children connect the concept with their own life experience
3) Ideas and activities to weave that concept into everyday life
4) Inspiring real-life stories about children who make a difference
5) Quotes from children, clergy, and community leaders, and others about the values of caring and compassion

In Part Three, you'll find additional chapters to support your efforts, with conversation starters, strategies to help your child relax, tips for troubleshooting challenging situations, and recommended books for adults and children interested in learning more.

There are so many ways to create meaningful connections with others. We've designed *The Kindness Advantage* to be used in whatever way works best for you and your family. For example, you can:

- Read the book for yourself, as a springboard for thinking about your own attitudes, experiences, and habits.
- Read the book from beginning to end and then discuss it with your child.
- Implement the suggestions that resonate with you.
- Scan the book for the parts that seem most relevant to your child's interests and personality.

You'll notice several blank pages at the end of the book for taking notes, writing questions, and keeping track of your resources. Our hope is that you will turn this book into your family's personal activity workbook.

Part One

Getting Started

Why Kindness?

No kind action ever stops with itself.
One kind action leads to another. Good example is followed.
A single act of kindness throws out roots in all directions,
and the roots spring up and make new trees.
The greatest work that kindness does to others is
that it makes them kind themselves.

—*Amelia Earhart, pilot*

Why kindness? That's a good question. Here's the short answer:
because kindness leads to a lot of other good things like compassion,
happiness, future success, better relationships, improved self-esteem,
and good mental and physical health. And don't we all want that for our
children, our families, and our community? In this chapter, we'll look at
the research that supports the specifics of the longer answer.

So how does nurturing kindness in our children make for happier kids, more harmonious homes, and a healthier society? As we will discuss further, empathy is one of the foundations for kindness. Empathy is the connection with another person that enables us to experience what he or she is thinking or feeling. Children as young as eight months old respond empathically when witnessing their mothers in distress. In one study, researchers reported: "all of the infants showed genuine empathy in emotional and cognitive ways."[1] In research-based community programs designed to foster social and emotional sensitivity in very young children, such as Roots of Empathy, empathy is taught by focusing on feelings of others. This important skill helps make for happier homes and families. Through these programs, families from different backgrounds get to spend time together in a natural way.

If you have been book shopping over the past several years you won't be surprised to know that the field of happiness is thriving. What you may not know is that psychologists have been studying happiness for many years.[2] In the last thirty or so years, these scientists have begun to examine what makes people happy, thrive, and flourish. "Research shows that performing positive activities such as expressing gratitude and doing acts of kindness boosts happiness."[3] Although much of this research has been with adults, children are now becoming the focus of more studies. One recent pioneering study with nine- to eleven-year-olds underscored the benefits to children who perform acts of kindness on a regular basis. The researchers found that these children, in addition to seeing positive changes in their academic experience, were more socially accepted. You could probably have guessed that those might be some of the benefits to the individual child; they are obvious. What may be less obvious is the benefit to their entire community. From engaging in acts of kindness, these children tend to be more inclusive and less likely to bully others as teenagers.[4] By nurturing our children to be kind, we are taking the first step in building happier, more harmonious communities.

Another study of kindness and happiness explores the "feedback loop" between them. "The practical implications of this positive feedback loop could be that engaging in one kind deed . . . would make you happier, and the happier you feel, the more likely you are to do another kind act."[5] Another version of this phenomenon is the "helper's high" first described by Allan Luks as "the powerful physical feelings people experience when directly helping others."[6] Three major aspects of the helper's high are the release of endorphins, a feeling of satisfaction, and overall improvement in physical and emotional health. Anyone who has done something kind for another person knows that it feels good. Now we have the science that tells us why.[7]

In various studies to support this, scientists notice changes in the brain when people think good thoughts, do kind acts themselves, or even observe other people performing kind acts. Endorphins or "feel good chemicals" are secreted in our brain; these secretions improve our mood. Another important hormone in this process, and one that is directly related to social connection, is oxytocin. It works in concert with serotonin, one of the endorphins released in the helper's high. "When it is operating during times of low stress, oxytocin physiologically rewards those who maintain good social bonds with feelings of well-being."[8] Another interesting aspect of this hormone is that when it is released during a stressful or painful time in someone's life "it may lead people to seek out more and better social contacts."[9] It is pretty amazing that we now know that when people are looking for ways to feel better when they are stressed or in pain, helping others will help them, too. Through

MRI scans, researchers can see that when you help someone, a specific region of your brain lights up. This gives you a feeling of "warm glow" that underscores the emotional benefits to kindness.

Did you know that volunteering could improve your health and help you live longer? A major government study of adults who volunteer found multiple benefits to physical and mental health such as improved cardiovascular function, increased sense of purpose and life satisfaction, and lower rates of depression.[10] According to statistics compiled by the National Philanthropic Trust, approximately 25 percent of the adult population in the United States volunteer with the top four areas being religious, educational, social service, and health organizations. Much of the research on volunteerism has been done with older adults, not surprising, since they often have more time.

The growing research on children in schools gives us insight into the positive effects they experience when helping others. Over the past twenty-five years, Service Learning (SL), has become a popular and meaningful way that students of all ages can become engaged in community service through their schools. Barbara Jacoby, a leader in the field of Service Learning, defines it as "a form of experiential education in which students engage in activities that address human and community needs together with structured opportunities for reflection designed to achieve desired learning outcomes."[11] There are positive results about the effects of service learning programs on young people. "Students participating in SL programs demonstrate significant gains in five outcome areas: attitudes toward self, attitudes toward school and learning, civic engagement, social skills, and academic performance. These findings bolster the views of educators who posit that SL programs can benefit students at different educational levels in several ways. These multiple benefits include such areas as enhanced self-efficacy and self-esteem, more positive attitudes toward school and education, an increase in positive attitudes and behaviors related to community involvement, and gains in social skills relating to leadership and empathy."[12] Students who experience these gains understand firsthand the value of kindness and connection which enables them to be contributing members of their communities. Sounds good to us!

There are so many reasons that kindness is important. At its essence, kindness allows us to develop awareness of and sensitivity to others. Having concern for others and being able to show that concern through our thoughts and actions will help us feel connected to those around us. This is not a new phenomenon. It was Charles Darwin, who, within the context of survival mechanisms, understood that we have an instinct to be sympathetic and caring."[13] To respond compassionately to someone else, we need to observe and understand what they are experiencing. In his book, *The Altruistic Brain*, Dr. Ronald Pfaff states, "how scientifically reasonable it can be to rely on the idea that we are wired from infancy to 'do the right thing'.[14] Even though we are hardwired for it, we need to work at it. With practice we can get really good at acting with kindness.

Do you remember the "Golden Rule"? Most of us, regardless of our different faiths and backgrounds, are taught this adage from a very early age. The Parliament of World Religions, the oldest, largest, and most inclusive convening organization of the global interfaith movement has opined on this topic. In 1993 they created their Declaration Toward a Global Ethic, a document that reiterates their commitment to the ideal of the golden rule. But how often do we actually ask ourselves, "How do I want to treat other people and how do I want to be treated?" At a time when we see so much rude behavior in the headlines and all around us, and targets of bullying are getting younger and younger, the world might be a better place if we asked that question more often. Kindness is really important now. And each act of kindness makes a difference.

Even the smallest gesture of kindness communicates to someone that we respect and value them. As we model kindness for our children, and offer them their own opportunities to practice it, they will become more open to and understanding of others. With this mindset we are more likely to meet and connect with different kinds of people creating bonds that might not have formed otherwise. This can work in both directions, with our openness attracting other people to us as well. The Buddhist monk and teacher Thich Nhat Hahn is often quoted as saying, "Compassion is a verb . . . Compassion and action go hand-in-hand." We look for ways to be compassionate, kind, and helpful so we can change the world and make it a better place. That is *The Kindness Advantage,* and as we discussed above, we are wired for it.

"Even three-month-old infants evaluate others based on their social behavior towards third parties."[15] Researchers at The Baby Lab at Yale University have conducted numerous studies with infants as young as three months old. Through a series of studies referred to as The Climber Studies, babies responded to "helpers" and "hinderers" who interacted with a character attempting to climb a hill. These infants showed a clear preference for the "helper" indicating their understanding of helping another in need. There is also evidence that toddlers feel good when they give to others. One study found "that before the age of two, toddlers exhibit greater happiness when giving treats to others than receiving treats themselves."[16]

In a different study of children of a similar age watching a familiar adult "playmate" who was playing with a teddy bear that became "injured," it was found that children "have access to the inner experience of other people, and they are socially competent to intervene in another's favor."[17] Isn't that remarkable? Clearly, these studies support the emotional preference for and desire to help that children experience from a very young age. "Studies suggest that perhaps kindness doesn't need to be taught anew as much as supported more continuously from an early age."[18] That is why we believe it is never too early to start modeling, reinforcing, and incorporating kindness into our everyday lives. The words of renowned psychologist and researcher Dr. Richard Davidson are compelling: "I would say from everything we know from a neuroscientific perspective, it's very important to begin as early as possible. We know that the brain is more plastic earlier in life. That is why it's easier for young children to learn a second language than it is for adults; it's why it's easier for young children to learn to play a musical instrument than it is for adults. Young children's brains are inherently more malleable; they're more flexible."[19]

Research has shown that in the chaos of daily life, while focusing on reinforcing their children's achievements, parents of preschoolers can miss their child's acts of kindness.[20] We will help you train yourself to be alert to those expressions of kindness that are so important and often missed. In addition, because we spend so much time with our young children we have a unique opportunity to set a positive example and nurture the foundation for kindness within our families. Being kind can make us feel good, help us feel connected to others, and give our life meaning. That is why taking action now will give your child *The Kindness Advantage.*

Setting a Positive Example

WE ARE ALL BORN WITH AN INNATE CAPACITY FOR LANGUAGE,
BUT THE EXPRESSION FOR LANGUAGE REQUIRES THAT WE BE RAISED
IN A LINGUISTIC COMMUNITY. AND SIMILARLY FOR KINDNESS
AND COMPASSION, WE ARE ALL BORN WITH THESE SEEDS,
BUT IT REQUIRES THAT THEY BE NURTURED, AND IF THEY'RE NOT
NURTURED, THEY WILL ATROPHY. AND SO ONE OF THE ROLES
OF CONTEMPORARY TRAINING IS TO NOURISH THESE SEEDS SO THAT
THEY DO BLOSSOM AND FLOURISH, AND THERE IS SCIENTIFIC
EVIDENCE TO SUGGEST THAT IT IS POSSIBLE.

*—Dr. Richard Davidson, psychologist on Upaya Conversations
podcast 802 "Innate Kindness" with Joanna Harcourt-Smith*

Want to help your kid develop a desire to help make the world a
better place? The best way to do that is to encourage, teach, and

demonstrate what it means to be kind to and care about others. Before you begin, it is important to reflect on your own life and understand what shaped your attitudes about caring. Read through and think about the questions below. When you are ready to write down your responses, these questions and room to write your answers are in the Journal Pages at the end of the book.

Are your attitudes about caring ones you want to pass down to your children or is it time to rethink them?

Think about when you were your child's age. Who do you remember being kind to you? What did they do? How did that make you feel?

When you think about someone kind and compassionate, who comes to mind? What did you observe them do? What did you learn from them? Were there ways you felt you could be like them? As you think about this person now, can you describe what makes them seem so kind?

When you were growing up, how did people in your family show that they cared for others?

Think about ways you showed kindness to others when you were a child. What did you do? How did other people respond?

Now that you are a parent, where is kindness demonstrated in your family's everyday life?

Describe ways you have seen other families demonstrate caring.

Where do you see room for more kindness in your everyday life?

Now that you have had a chance to reflect on where some of your own attitudes have come from, you're ready to focus on your child. Here are some ideas to keep in mind as you move forward.

Start at Home

THE MOST INFLUENTIAL OF ALL EDUCATIONAL FACTORS
IS THE CONVERSATION IN A CHILD'S HOME.

—*William Temple, bishop*

What starts a conversation about helping others? Anything can. Let the conversation unfold naturally. It could be a news story that touches you, or your child may come home from school with a question or concern about something that happened that day. Listen and respond positively and without judgment when children bring their observations to you. You can create an environment where everyone, adults and kids alike, is encouraged to share ideas and question what they observe. By doing this, you will help your child become aware of the needs in their school or community. This awareness may be the first step to becoming involved.

When your child is engaged in an activity or project at school, use it as an opportunity to discuss what and whose need is being met by their efforts. Ask questions. "How is what you're doing making a difference?" When he talks to you about something he's seen that concerns him, you can ask, "Can you think of something you can do about that?" and "Is there a way I can help you?" Remember, we are all in a position to help others and these experiences are part of *The Kindness Advantage*.

Your Child Is Listening

Words convey our attitudes and feelings about others and the way we view the world. There are many differences among people, including race, ethnicity, religion, socioeconomic status, sexual orientation, physical, and mental differences. How do you talk about people who are "different" from you or your family? Many of us focus more on how we are *different from,* rather than *similar to* others. Be conscious of the language you use when describing people. You may not even be aware of the impact the things you say about others has on your child.

Similarly, the way you express a feeling you have about a situation, whether you are discouraged or hopeful, impacts your child. If you talk about problems as insurmountable, your child is less likely to feel his or her efforts will make a difference. If you have a positive attitude about helping, and are hopeful, your child is more likely to feel encouraged and have a sense that change is possible. The point is that children will develop their own ideas in great part based on what they hear you say.

Your Child Is Watching

You are a model for your child. In your everyday life, your child will watch how you treat others, when you hold the door for someone behind you or offer to help someone carry a heavy bag. Additionally, show your child what it means to dedicate your time and effort to a cause or project that is important to you. Find something you care about and enjoy. You may volunteer to do something on your own or with others. Either way, your child can see the benefit. You can stuff envelopes for a fundraiser, serve meals at a soup kitchen, walk dogs at a shelter, or collect clothes for hurricane victims. Often, the recipient of your effort may not even be aware of what you are doing. Explain to your child that sometimes you do things without being recognized. Whatever you choose, the important thing is that your child is aware of *what* you do and *why* you do it. If possible, bring your child with you to see you in action. If you can't do that, then share photos and stories about your experiences. In addition to watching you, your child is watching other people. These may be neighbors, family members, or celebrities. Expand your conversations to include what these people are doing to make a difference. Think back to the types of people who came to mind when you thought about a kind, compassionate person in your life and share one or two of those stories with your child.

Talking to Your Child About Books, Movies, and TV

Reading a book or watching a TV show or movie together offers great opportunities to start a dialogue. Talking about the dilemmas characters face and the choices they make can provide the framework for a natural conversation about values. Some books, shows, and movies will help you talk to your child about making kindness and caring part of everyday life. Others might serve as an example of when kindness is lacking or meanness takes the lead. When you look at the world through a lens of kindness, you will find many opportunities to observe and point out different behaviors. Taking the time to comment is good practice; you'll find that this close observation becomes second nature. When you model asking these questions and analyze the world in this way, your child will learn to do the same. This will help her have the kindness advantage.

Asking questions and making comments will help you access the ideas you want to highlight. As you talk, you may find that your child misses some of the subtleties that you hope to discuss. If so, explain them before continuing with the conversation. Here are a few universal topics to think about as you get started. Feel free to ask some of the questions below or come up with your own.

- **Motivation:** What makes characters do what they do or say what they say? What is behind their action? When you ask, "What were they thinking or how were they feeling when they said or did that?" you can talk about how the character might feel in a particular situation.

- **Choices:** With many choices for how to behave, why do characters choose to behave **this** way? When you ask, "Why do you think they did that?" or, "Why do you think they said that?" or, "Why do you think they chose not to do anything?" you can talk about what influences the choices a character makes.

- **Context and Influences:** Consider the many factors that influence characters' behavior. And remember, they may behave differently in different situations. When you ask, "Would he have said that in front of his mom? Did he behave differently because he was with his friends?" or, "Would she have taken that toy that didn't belong to her if her sister hadn't lost her doll?" or, "Would she have the confidence to stand up for herself if she had done it before?," it will give you a way into talking about how context and being around different people influence behavior.

- **Impact/Consequences:** What happens to characters when they do or say something? How do their actions impact them? How about the other characters? What

changes? When you ask, "If that character did something different, how would the friendship be different?"
or, "How do you think that character feels about herself
after saying what she said?" or, "What turned out well (or
badly) as a result of what that character did?," this is an
opportunity to talk about the impact of our behavior in
general. Examining these outcomes can help our children
develop empathy.

- **Relatability**: In what ways are the characters' experiences
familiar? When you ask, "Have you ever felt that way?"
or, "How do you think you would handle it if you were in
the same situation?" or, "Can you think of anyone who
did something similar to what the character did?" it will
help your child connect the events you've read about or
watched to their own life.

Now It Is Your Child's Turn

Every kid can be kind and every kid can do something. Help your
child become involved in a way that is appropriate to his or her age and
emotional development. Remember, every experience is important.

- There are kids who use their interests or talents to help others.
- There are kids who give away or sell their own things to benefit others.
- There are kids who let their passions guide them when helping others.
- There are kids who spend their time building relationships
with others.

What would your child like to do? Follow her lead or suggest something you think would interest her. Some of the most impactful volunteer projects are those envisioned and created by caring children. We can help our children discover *their* own path and create their own plans.

Research shows that those who keep track of their own acts of kindness towards others are more likely to be grateful and happier and do more acts of kindness.[1] Noticing acts of kindness in everyday life takes practice. Some acts are obvious and others we take for granted. Ask your child to tell you when people were kind to her that day. This may lead to conversations about how that kindness made her feel. After a few days of doing this, your child will likely become more aware of both big and small acts of kindness. Next, have your child count the acts of kindness she does each day. An easy way to do this is to have your child make a chart, put it on the refrigerator, and count and record each act of kindness she performs over the course of a week. Talk with your child about how she felt when she was kind and, if that kindness was towards another person, how she thinks that person felt.

Now we're ready to learn the fundamentals of kindness. They are:

- Acceptance
- Commitment
- Connection
- Empathy
- Giving
- Interest
- Nurturing
- Observing
- Questioning
- (be) Yourself

Part Two

Take It In

The Fundamentals of Kindness

➠ **Acceptance**

> WHEN I SEE YOU THROUGH MY EYES,
> I THINK WE ARE DIFFERENT. WHEN I SEE YOU THROUGH
> MY HEART, I KNOW WE ARE THE SAME.
>
> —*Doe Zantamata, author and artist*

For You to Read:

Accepting others as they are means seeing and hearing them without a filter of judgment. We owe that same courtesy to ourselves. It is easier to accept others as they are when we accept ourselves as we are. When we accept, we become more open to exchanging ideas and customs with others, which helps bring us together. When it comes to traditions or lifestyle, if we make an effort to learn about people, we can better appreciate the way they live, even when their practices are different from our own. Our focus is on finding ways to relate to each other rather than keeping our distance. We are aware of differences—we acknowledge them and how they contribute to our uniqueness—but we do not allow them to interfere with acceptance.

To Read with Your Child:

Everybody is different. People have different color hair, eyes, and skin, favorite foods, favorite sports, and so on and that doesn't make them better or worse...just different. Think about your best friend or brother or sister. You're probably different in lots of ways, but there's also a lot you have in common. Do you get stuck on all of the differences, or do you accept them for who they are? Sometimes, the differences between people are the best part of a friendship. Try to do the same thing with people you don't know—accept them. Learning more about people and how they live can help you become more accepting.

- Think about a way one of your friends is different from you. How does this difference make it hard for you to be friends? Or does it?
- What is a way you and a friend are similar or alike?
- Have you met anyone who you think is too different from you to be your friend? Why?

What Parents Can Do:

- Make connections with people who are different from you— different religions, races, and backgrounds. Make an effort to assure that your child knows a diverse group of your friends and colleagues.

- Find local festivals or celebrations of holidays that your family doesn't observe. Try to attend. Use them as opportunities to learn about others' customs.
- Read your child books about children or families in other countries or cultures.
- Listen to music from other cultures.

What Kids Can Do:

- "Interview" another person. Find out where she was born, what her favorite food is, and how many children are in her family.
- Try a food that a friend likes that you have never tried before.
- Do an activity with someone who you don't know very well.
- Have you met people who live in another city, state, or country? Use a map to mark where they are from.
- Learn to say "Hello" in another language.

Real-LIFE
Story 1

Sarah's brother has disabilities. She noticed that he was often left out of sports teams and clubs and did not get to do fun things with other kids. Sarah realized there were a lot of other teenagers in the same situation as her brother. They needed to be a part of an activity with other kids. Sarah loved cheerleading and dancing. She started an "inclusive"* cheerleading squad in her high school so girls with disabilities like her brother could join in. The girls practiced well together but she was worried the day of the first game. Would the whole school welcome this special team? They did! Because of this experience, Sarah decided to start an organization, called The Sparkle Effect, to help other high school cheerleading teams do the same thing. To find out more, visit www.thesparkleeffect.org.

This is when kids with and without disabilities are part of the same team, club, or classroom.

WHEN WE FINISHED PERFORMING,
THE ENTIRE STADIUM FULL OF SPECTATORS ROSE
TO THEIR FEET AND BEGAN TO CHEER. AT THAT MOMENT,
I REALIZED THAT THIS UNPRECEDENTED AND UNLIKELY SQUAD
WAS GOING TO CHANGE MY HIGH SCHOOL FOREVER.

—Sarah Cronk,
creator of The Sparkle Effect

 Real-LIFE Story 2 When Matthew was in eighth grade his younger brother became the target of cyberbullying. Matthew watched as his brother transformed from an outgoing and happy boy to one who was sad and reluctant to engage with other kids. Matthew realized the intense negative power of bullying and decided to do something.

He began the Be ONE project, which stands for "Be Open to New Experiences." It was, initially, a short, interactive anti-bullying presentation with group activities that he presented to his brother's sixth grade class. Because the program was successful, he was asked to offer it to others. As described on their website, the program "not only challenges kids to be kind, but to be positive role models who hold others accountable to be kind as well, thereby harnessing the power of peer pressure towards inclusiveness, rather than exclusiveness." This idea is fundamental to acceptance. Since it began, the Be ONE project has grown to reach thousands of middle school students in several states. To find out more, visit www.thebeoneproject.org.

IT'S FINDING WAYS ON YOUR OWN THAT
YOU CAN HELP REPAIR YOUR SMALL COMMUNITY IN
YOUR LITTLE CORNER OF THE WORLD.

—Matthew Kaplan,
founder of the Be ONE Project

⠿➤ Commitment

> IT IS NOT ENOUGH TO UNDERSTAND, OR
> TO SEE CLEARLY. THE FUTURE WILL BE SHAPED IN THE
> ARENA OF HUMAN ACTIVITY, BY THOSE WILLING TO COMMIT
> THEIR MIND AND THEIR BODIES TO THE TASK.
>
> —*Robert Kennedy, American politician*

For You to Read:

What does it take to make a commitment to making kindness a way of life for you and your family? There is the theory and the practice. Most of us agree with the idea of being kind to others, the challenge is acting on it when given a chance. Just knowing that there will be opportunities to be kind is an important first step in your commitment. It is up to us to notice those opportunities. Each of us can commit to doing acts of kindness based on what we encounter in the world each day. Being kind involves your whole being: body, mind, and heart. Sometimes it feels terrific to be kind, other times it can be a challenge. Just be aware of this. Although it may be easier to see the opportunities to choose kindness when you're alone, try not to ignore them when you're with your child. That way, your child will learn to put this idea into practice, too.

To Read with Your Child:

Being kind has three parts: noticing, thinking, and doing. First, you notice what is going on: Does that dog look lost? Is someone being mean to that girl? Is your brother sad? Next, you think about what would be a kind thing to do in that situation. Then, you figure out a way to do it. When you practice being kind, it becomes easier.

What Kids Can Do:

- If you see another child walk away and forget something, like their sweatshirt, pick it up and bring it to them.
- When you know you're going to a duck pond, bring bread to feed the ducks.
- If you see an empty potato chip bag as you're walking, pick it up and put it in a trash can.
- You notice that your sister falls asleep on the couch. Cover her with a blanket so she doesn't get cold.
- When a friend's sandwich drops on the floor, offer to share half of yours. Even if it is your favorite lunch, and you might not really want to share it, it is a kind thing to do.

What Parents Can Do:

- If you're out without your child and observe an act of kindness, when you come home, tell your child what you saw and why it touched you.
- You're late getting home from work and your child is upset. Explain that you saw someone whose car had a flat tire and took extra time to help them.
- You and your child are at the supermarket. You notice a shopper rudely push past someone who is slower moving their cart. Talk to your child about this encounter. Would it have been kinder for the rushed shopper to wait or politely say, "Excuse me?"
- You have made a commitment to help people who are hungry. If you have an errand to run and know that it is near a local shelter, take a little extra time to pack a bag of canned food with your child. Deliver it when you're in the neighborhood.

- While you and your child are riding home on a crowded bus, you notice a pregnant woman get on. Stand up and offer her your seat. Be sure to explain to your child why you did that.

When she was nine years old, Neha visited an orphanage in India with her family, as was their tradition. When she returned home to Pennsylvania, she wanted to find a way to help the children she had met. She was moved and motivated by the tremendous differences between her life and the lives of the orphans. Neha accepted that the children did not have parents or guidance but knew that without education and access to health care, they would remain living in poverty. In an effort to change that, Neha founded a charitable organization to help orphans in India. By the time she was fifteen, the charity already had a life-changing impact on those children and had built libraries, computer labs, sewing centers and hosted eye, dental, and vaccination clinics. To date, the charity Neha founded has helped 30,000 orphans. To find out more, visit www. empowerorphans.org.

> I GOT STARTED WITH A SMALL GARAGE SALE,
> THINKING ON A NINE YEAR OLD SCALE. I GATHERED ALL MY
> TOYS WHEN I GOT BACK FROM INDIA AND PUT THEM IN THE
> DRIVEWAY AND WE ORGANIZED A GARAGE SALE.
>
> —*Neha Gupta, founder of Empower Orphans*

From the time he was two years old, Max went along with his parents who volunteered at a soup kitchen. Looking for his own volunteer opportunity when he was seven, Max realized there were no places that would welcome children his age. He decided to begin his own charity to encourage other kids to "give back" and to volunteer in their community. Max heard about a local homeless shelter that would be happy to welcome young volunteers. Since he started, the 30–40 homeless kids at the shelter have enjoyed pizza and dance parties, ice cream, socials, trips to a local sports complex, and sleepovers, all thanks to Max and the 200 volunteers he recruited. Those volunteers, all children, do a variety of things for the children at the shelter. Some have led reading groups, run chess clubs, organized Thanksgiving dinner (even renting tablecloths and china to make it more special), and one volunteer taught a little girl to play the violin. To find out more, visit www.happykidscarect.com.

> EVERY CHILD IN THIS WORLD IS SPECIAL.
> I WANT TO MAKE SURE THEY ALL FEEL THAT WAY.
>
> —*Max Konzerosky, founder of HappyKidsCare*

➠ Connection

> WHEN WE KNOW OURSELVES TO BE CONNECTED TO
> ALL OTHERS, ACTING COMPASSIONATELY IS
> SIMPLY THE NATURAL THING TO DO.
>
> —*Dr. Rachel Naomi Remen, author, medical educator*

For You to Read:

When we bring people together, we have the opportunity to create a connection between ourselves and someone, something, or someplace else. Making connections with others and sharing ideas is the foundation for a meaningful relationship. We as parents should remember the power of the way we speak and think about people who are not like us. By watching us, our children can learn that connecting with someone is about paying attention, listening, watching, and being "there." If we speak negatively about others, our children can also be influenced. In this case, it might discourage them from exploring these relationships. Despite language, culture, neighborhood, or physical differences, we have the ability to connect with anyone because at our core we are the same.

To Read with Your Child:

Think about a bridge. What is it? A bridge is a connection from one place to another. There are lots of ways to connect with others. Think about your family, your neighborhood, and the bigger world around you. We can connect with people we meet, or groups of people who are doing something that we like to do, too. Another way to connect with people is to become part of a program or organization doing something that interests us. Connecting with different people helps us think about things in a new way and that can be fun.

- Name three people you feel a connection with. What makes you feel connected to them?
- Who has tried to connect with you? What did they do?
- We can feel connected to places and people. Think about a place in your neighborhood that you visit—it could be a park, library, community center, or someplace else. What makes you feel connected to that place?

What Parents Can Do:

- Invite an older relative over to cook a special recipe for a particular holiday.
- Talk to your child about three ways you are connected with other people or groups of people.

- Tell your child about your new friend or colleague. Share the reasons why you are interested in getting to know them better (connecting) and how you're going to do it.
- Share holidays with a family who has different traditions than yours.

What Kids Can Do:

- Maybe there is a new kid on your soccer team. You can be a bridge between your two families. They could meet and might even become friends because of you.
- Connect with someone at school by asking them to sit next to you.
- You can also connect with people in your own family. Play with a younger cousin or look at a photo album with your grandmother.

Real-LIFE
Story 1

When Kayla was eleven years old, her father was diagnosed with brain cancer. Sadly, he died five months later. During the time her dad was sick, Kayla often came home from school frustrated because it seemed like everyone knew about breast cancer—the month (October), the color (pink), the events (Race For The Cure), the symbol (pink ribbon)—but none of her friends knew anything about brain cancer. Since her mother did not have a good answer as to why this was the case, Kayla decided to look for organizations that help brain cancer patients and their families. She found one that did just that. Almost a year after her dad died, on her twelfth birthday, Kayla and her friends walked in the first walk-a-thon hosted by this organization. For several weeks before the walk Kayla asked friends, family, neighbors, and teachers to sponsor her. When emailing or talking to people, Kayla told them about her family's experience with brain cancer. Even though she was terribly sad that her dad had died, talking to people about him made her feel better. Everyone she spoke to about the walk-a-thon became connected to the organization. As a way to thank her for her hard work and fundraising the following year, Kayla was named "teen ambassador." At their second walk-a-thon, she was publicly recognized and received an award for her efforts to raise awareness and money that helps other families affected by brain cancer.

 Mira, Ade, and Ayanna are cousins who are string musicians. Using their musical talents to inspire other children, they began performing together when they were six, seven, and twelve years old, respectively. They play classical music, and in addition to performing professionally, they make an effort to bring music to hospitals, libraries, and schools, where many music programs have been cut. For many children, attending one of these concerts is their first experience hearing live music. Hearing the girls perform is transformative for some children.

> OUR MAIN GOAL, SINCE WE ARE YOUNG,
> BLACK AND FEMALE MUSICIANS . . . TO TARGET TOWARDS
> YOUNGER KIDS . . . WE SEEM TO INSPIRE KIDS TO START LEARNING
> STRING INSTRUMENTS AND INSTRUMENTS IN GENERAL.
>
> —*Ayanna Williams*

⟶ Empathy

> EMPATHY IS THE ACCURATE UNDERSTANDING
> OF ANOTHER PERSON'S INTERNAL EXPERIENCE. IT HAS NOTHING
> TO DO WITH AGREEING OR DISAGREEING WITH THAT EXPERIENCE.
> UNLIKE SYMPATHY, IT MAKES NO ASSUMPTIONS ABOUT
> HOW THE OTHER PERSON IS FEELING.
>
> —*Dr. Madeline Levine, psychologist*

For You to Read:

When you attempt to understand someone else's experience, you are being empathic. Listening carefully and watching closely helps you develop empathy because you put your own reactions aside to focus on the other person's experience. Although we do not know firsthand exactly what someone else is feeling or thinking, we can try to understand their situation from both our head and our heart. Hopefully, then, because we become sensitive to what that person wants or needs, our responses will be meaningful to them. Remember, what you need is not necessarily what another person would need in the same situation.

The best way to teach your child empathy is to be empathic. Be open to the range of emotions your child expresses. Be aware of your reaction so that you do not impede their emotional response. Some feelings are comfortable and others uncomfortable, but all feelings are normal. You can help your child navigate the feelings they are having. Our emotional responses are an important part of what makes us human and connects us with others so that we can see the world through their eyes. That is empathy.

To Read with Your Child:

Isn't it fun to imagine things? You might imagine what you're going to do when you grow up or that you have super powers. Empathy is like a game of imagination. You imagine what another person might be feeling and thinking in a particular situation. Then you will have an idea of what they might want you to say or do to help them. Empathy can help you feel closer to others and let other people know you care.

• Think about a time someone knew how you were feeling without being told. How do you think they knew? Can you describe what they did or said? Did that help you to feel better?

- What are clues you can look for to understand how another person is feeling?
- If you saw a classmate crying on the playground, what do you think she might want you to do? What would you want someone to do or say if you were crying on the playground?

What Parents Can Do:

- If you see a hurt bird, stop and talk to your child about how to help. You could call an animal rescue hotline. You might put the bird in a shoebox and take it to a veterinary office or animal hospital.
- When you're watching a movie or TV show with your child, talk about how one of the characters might be feeling and how you would feel in that situation.
- A sibling or relative is playing in a music recital. Congratulate him and share his excitement for his accomplishment.
- If you're taking time to talk with a friend about a challenging situation, explain to your child what you're doing and why. You don't have to share the details, but do let your child know that you're listening to your friend and trying to help.

What Kids Can Do:

- You have a friend whose toy broke and you have the same one; share it with her.
- There is a new boy at your school who you see alone at recess. Ask him if he wants to play with you.

- Your sister tells you she is sad. Ask her why, and listen carefully to her answer.

Real-LIFE
Story 1

Lots of children like to put on shows. Usually they do it after dinner, for their family, or in the basement with their friends. Abigail took entertaining others to a different level. In honor of her great grandmother's 100th birthday, Abigail, seven years old, wanted "to sing some songs for her at her home (an assisted living center). I noticed how the elderly appreciated my performances so I thought it'd be a great idea to form a group so we could do a whole show for them. That's when I discovered many of the elderly didn't have visitors." Abigail invited friends to perform with her at assisted-living residences, nursing homes, and children's hospitals. Her goal was "to brighten up people's days and help them have a fun time; if I do my best, they'll have a smile on their faces by the end." Abigail gathered a talented group of thirteen girls ages six to thirteen, who sing a selection of more than ninety Broadway and pop songs. To find out more, visit www.caregirlz.org.

Real-LIFE
Story 2

When Peter was six years old, he and his Cub Scout troop slept out in a tent to help raise awareness and funds to fight homelessness. They were inspired by a man in their Minnesota community named Bob Fischer, who slept outside every night of the holiday season for many years with that same mission. "I was only in first grade," Peter said, "but when Bob said that $500 could keep a family in their home for a month, I thought, 'Hey! I can do that.'" Although Peter didn't meet his fund-raising goal that first year, he continued sleeping in just a cardboard box in the Minnesota winter for much of November and all of December year after year.

By the time he was seventeen, Peter had raised over $400,000, which has helped over 1,000 families stay in their homes. He has also inspired hundreds of others, both in his community and beyond, to join the fight against homelessness.

> I SLEEP OUT BECAUSE, IN MY HEART, I KNOW
> I'M HELPING OTHER PEOPLE.
>
> —*Peter Larson*

Giving

> SINCE YOU GET MORE JOY OUT OF GIVING JOY TO OTHERS,
> YOU SHOULD PUT A GOOD DEAL OF THOUGHT INTO
> THE HAPPINESS THAT YOU ARE ABLE TO GIVE.
>
> —*Eleanor Roosevelt, politician, diplomat, activist*

For You to Read:

Research shows that people who give to others are happier and healthier than those who do not. Giving creates a positive response in our brain, which has been referred to as a "helper's high," which we discussed in Chapter 1. The benefits are both physical and mental, underscoring the expression "it's better to give than to receive." There are lots of ways to give. Some people chose to give money, some material goods. All of us can give of ourselves whether it is our time, talent, or expertise. By giving to others and teaching our children to do so we are laying the foundation for their future happiness and health. Sharing the joy of giving with our children and making them a part of the experience of enhancing others' lives gives them a unique feeling of connection and purpose.

To Read with Your Child:

There are lots of ways that you can give to others. You can give things, your time, or you can share what you're good at. You can even just give someone a smile and see what you get in return. When you do something that is helpful it usually makes you feel good. You're making a difference.

- What are things you like to do that you can share with other people? Think about things you do with your friends and family.
- Think of a situation when someone gave you something that made a difference in your life. What was it?
- What are two of the best gifts (not material things) that you have ever received?

What Parents Can Do:

- Gather clothes to give away. Spend time going through your closet and help your child do the same. Include your child in deciding where these clothes will go. You might even take your child with you when you drop off the donation.
- If your child loves to draw, encourage him to turn some of the drawings into cards for people who are in the hospital.
- Volunteer your time and talk about your experience with your child. Share with her why you go to this specific place and the reason it is important to you.

What Kids Can Do:

- If you play the piano, play at your local senior center.
- Bake your favorite cookies for a friend who is sick.
- Teach someone to jump rope.

- Give clothes you've outgrown that are still in good shape to a smaller cousin or friend.

 After seeing the Gulf of Mexico oil spill reported on TV, eleven-year-old artist Olivia was motivated to help. As a fundraiser, Olivia created 500 original watercolor illustrations of birds. Anyone who made a donation to the Audubon society received one of her watercolors. Olivia's efforts raised over $200,000. Olivia's illustrations are showcased in a book that she wrote, and a portion of the proceeds are donated to Gulf Coast cleanup efforts. To find out more, visit www.oliviabouler.net.

> WHEN I FIRST HEARD ABOUT THE OIL SPILL IT WAS
> SO DEVASTATING MY DAD WAS TALKING TO MY GRANDPARENTS
> WHO LIVE ON THE GULF IN ALABAMA ABOUT THREE DAYS
> AFTER IT HAPPENED. WE DISCUSSED IT AT THE DINNER TABLE AND
> I STARTED CRYING. I TOLD EVERYBODY THAT I HAVE TO
> MAKE A DIFFERENCE FOR THOSE BIRDS. I RAN UPSTAIRS AND
> WROTE A LETTER TO AUDUBON. I SAID I WANT TO USE MY ABILITY
> TO DRAW TO RAISE MONEY FOR BIRDS IN THE GULF.

—*Olivia Bouler, author of* Olivia's Birds: Saving The Gulf

 In 2004, when Brittany was twelve years old and her brother Robbie was thirteen, they heard a news story about a soldier returning from Iraq with a huge phone bill. Upset to hear about this soldier's debt, they collected money and opened a bank account with the goal of paying this soldier's phone bill. The bank manager was so impressed with the teens that he added an additional $500, which motivated them even more. They knew that if they could help this one soldier, they could probably help many others, too, which was the idea behind their charity. After holding several other fundraisers, Brittany and Robbie decided to collect and recycle used cell phones, using the proceeds to buy prepaid phone cards for the troops serving overseas. Since starting their charity they have provided more than 300 million minutes of free talk time and recycled more than 11 million cell phones. To find out more, visit www.cellphonesforsoldiers.com.

> WE HEARD THE STORY OF A SOLDIER RETURNING FROM IRAQ WITH AN ALMOST $8,000 PHONE BILL. OUR COUSIN HAD RECENTLY BEEN DEPLOYED AND THE STORY REALLY HIT HOME FOR BOTH OF US.
>
> HOW COULD A MAN WHO WAS SERVING HIS COUNTRY NOT BE ABLE TO CALL HIS FAMILY FOR FREE? HE WAS SACRIFICING SO MUCH FOR ALL OF US. ROBBIE AND I DECIDED TO DO SOMETHING. WE CLEANED OUT OUR PIGGY BANK, GATHERED LUNCH MONEY, AND EVEN HELD A CAR WASH TO TRY TO HELP THIS ONE MAN.
>
> —*Brittany Bergquist,*
> *co-founder of Cell Phones for Soldiers*

➠ Interest

> A MAN WHO LIMITS HIS INTEREST, LIMITS HIS LIFE.
>
> —*Vincent Price, actor*

For You To Read:

Interests can be driven by curiosity or a feeling we get when we explore something we care about. It is normal for children to have varied interests that change and evolve over time. Their age, friends, experiences, and environment are just some aspects of their life that may guide those interests. Childhood is a time for exploration and wonder. Some of your child's interests will be short lived; others will take root. If your child is curious about something, encourage him to learn more. You never know when an interest will turn into a passion. For some of us, pursuing an interest gives purpose to our lives. For your child, it may be an interest that motivates him to help someone or do something and become part of something greater than himself.

To Read with Your Child:

We are all interested in things. Discover what excites you or what you're good at and go for it! You can explore interests on your own. You can practice and do your own research: read, ask questions, talk to people, or watch videos to learn more. You might join a club, go to a library or museum to learn more and meet other people who are interested in the same thing. Teaching someone about what you love is a great way to share your interest. Whatever you decide, stay enthusiastic; you never know where your interest might take you.

What Parents Can Do:

- Encourage your child to be curious. That curiosity might lead to an interest that can bring him joy.
- How do you explore your own interests? Describe that process to your child. If you're a knitter, show your child the pattern you're following and the needles and yarn you've chosen. And of course, if he's interested, invite him to sit with you and watch you knit. If one of the things you do with your knitting is to make hats for soldiers, be sure he knows.
- As your child discovers his own passions, help him find ways to use them to contribute to the world.

- Look for opportunities that allow you to pursue interests as a family. If you're all interested in the topic of hunger, you might plan a family visit to a food pantry or soup kitchen.

What Children Can Do:

- If you're interested in cats, go to the library and check out two books about them to learn more.
- Practice your magic tricks for a friend after school.
- Watch a video biography about one of your favorite athletes.
- Teach your brother how to draw the dog that you love to draw.
- Interview an older relative like your grandmother or great uncle if you're interested in your family history.

Real-LIFE
Story 1

Nine-year-old Austin saw a video featuring children who'd lost their parents to HIV and AIDS. Learning that every fourteen seconds a child was orphaned because of HIV/AIDS, Austin realized that 2,057 kids are orphaned during each school day. Wanting to help, he held a shoot-a-thon on World AIDS Day and raised $3,000. Today, Austin sponsors events where thousands of people in more than twenty-five countries shoot baskets for donations. To date, he has raised nearly $4 million, which goes toward clothing, food, shelter, medicine, and education for children in Africa and India who are orphaned due to HIV/AIDS. To find out more, visit www.austingutwein.com.

As a nine-year-old, I didn't know what I could do to make a difference . . . so I was encouraged to start something and to use my favorite sport to make a difference. I decided to shoot baskets and raise money; kind of like a WALK-A-THON.

—*Austin Gutwein*

When Chandra was six years old, she was homeless, living in a tent with her mother and her dog in Colorado. She ate at soup kitchens where there were no healthy fruits or vegetables. Chandra gained weight and was pre-diabetic. Seven years later, when she and her mother were back on their feet, Chandra thought of a way to provide fruits and vegetables for homeless people. By collecting pennies in jugs placed throughout the community, she raised money to support organic gardens. "There is a lot of pennies everywhere. You can find them on the ground." Her goal was to provide fresh produce to 1,000 homeless people during the growing season.

> WE LEARNED THAT WE CAN HANDLE ANYTHING
> IF WE JUST HAVE THE COURAGE AND
> STRENGTH TO GET THROUGH IT.
>
> —*Chandra Starr*

⁛➡ Nurturing

> THE GREATEST COMPLIMENT THAT WAS
> EVER PAID ME WAS WHEN SOMEONE ASKED ME WHAT
> I THOUGHT, AND ATTENDED TO MY ANSWER.
>
> —*Henry David Thoreau*

For You to Read:

Nurturing makes a person feel that someone cares. When we nurture our children they feel secure and encouraged. We can also model and teach them the importance of taking care of ourselves. By eating well, being physically active, getting enough sleep, and having quiet time or downtime, we are showing our children ways to do this. Science shows us that our children benefit when they are nurtured and nurture themselves. Hopefully, in turn, they will want to nurture others, which allows them to experience the positive effect that results from caring for someone else.

Throughout the day, we have countless opportunities to nurture relationships with people, and even animals and plants, just by noticing and doing something. Try hugging your child (because he is there, not because he did something), "pinching back" a plant, or bringing coffee to a coworker. The everyday, simple kindnesses that sometimes slip our minds are most often what is at the core of a well-nurtured relationship.

To Read with Your Child:

When you care for someone or something over time you are being nurturing. There are lots of ways we can nurture other living things. You are being nurturing when you listen to your neighbor's stories because you are showing that you're interested in him and what he has to say. When you offer to share a snack with a friend, you are nurturing her by being generous and making sure she has something to eat. When you water your plant or feed your fish, you are providing it with what it needs to survive, which is also a form of nurturing.

- Can you think of a time when someone did something nurturing for you? What did he do? How did that make you feel? Did you nurture someone else in a similar way?
- Can you think of something different you could do to nurture a friend?
- What are two ways you can nurture yourself?

What Parents and Kids Can Do:

Think about ways you can be kind or nurturing throughout the day. Here are some ideas:

- Look at someone as you say hello to him.
- Hold the door for someone entering a room behind you.
- Ask a friend how she is and listen carefully to her answer.
- Smile and say hello to someone you see regularly. It may be your bus driver or the crossing guard.
- If you see your grandpa is fixing his car, or your sister has just played a soccer game, ask them to tell you about it. People often like to talk about things that they enjoy doing. When they are asked to do that, they feel nurtured.

When Zach was six years old, Hurricane Charley struck near his home in Florida. He wanted to help people whose homes had been badly damaged or destroyed in the hurricane. Zach walked around his neighborhood with his wagon collecting supplies for a nearby shelter. Zach's mom wanted him to see how helpful the supplies he collected were to the people who needed them. So she took him to the shelter. This visit got Zach excited about doing more to help people. The next year, he started a charity that puts together backpacks filled with toothbrushes, toothpaste, soap, shampoo, school supplies, food, and toys for children who are homeless or in families that don't have enough money to buy those things. Zach kept visiting shelters to meet some of the people he helped. Over the years, Zach has distributed over 10,000 backpacks to homeless kids across America. In addition to his backpack project, as a way to raise awareness about childhood homelessness, Zach walked nearly 2,500 miles across the United States.

WHEN I WOULD SEE THESE SHELTERS AND
WHAT THESE KIDS WERE GOING THROUGH THAT REALLY
INSPIRED ME TO GROW THE FOUNDATION
INTO WHAT IT IS TODAY.

—*Zach Bonner, creator of Little Red Wagon Foundation*

Real-LIFE
Story 2

Soon after the devastating earthquake in Haiti, twelve-year-old Blare saw a news story with a little boy crying in the ruins of a building. He cried, too. "I kind of wanted to give him a hug and I was kind of thinking that he could be my brother." Blare asked his mom if they could do anything for the kids who suffered in the earthquake. He remembered that it was his teddy bear that brought him comfort when he was scared so he decided to start a teddy bear drive for kids in Haiti. At school, he announced his plan and asked other students to donate bears. Local TV and radio stations heard about the drive, and, using Facebook the word spread and students in other schools donated bears as well. Blare has now collected over 50,000 bears. Now he has expanded his reach and is collecting many different supplies for kids in Haiti.

IT DOESN'T REALLY MATTER HOW SMALL OR OLD YOU ARE . . .
IF YOU'RE YOUNG AND THINK YOU CAN'T MAKE
A BIG DIFFERENCE IN THE WORLD,
WELL, YOU ACTUALLY CAN.

—*Blare Gooch, founder of Blare's Bears for Haiti*

⟶ Observing

YOU CAN OBSERVE A LOT BY WATCHING.

—*Yogi Berra, baseball player, manager, and coach*

For You to Read:

When you have your eyes open to the world around you, you can interpret what you see for your child. This will shape the way your child sees the world and likely encourage his curiosity about different ways he can interact with it. It is important to expose him, in an age appropriate way, to aspects of life that are challenging. With a little practice, you can talk with your child about anything. Although it is a natural instinct for parents, shielding your child from difficult topics precludes conversation and knowledge about various issues and conditions in the world. Approaching these topics provides necessary opportunities for observation. And don't we all want our children to become keen observers?

To Read With Your Child:

The world is an amazing place! There is so much to see when you pay attention: the colors, the sounds, the tastes, and more. Wherever you are, use your senses to observe what is around you. Some things will be familiar and others will be less so. Notice what people are doing. It is a good chance to discover new things. Your observations may make you think or act in a different way.

What Parents Can Do:

- When you are out walking around with your child, be present. Comment on things you observe, and be aware of how it might start a conversation. Resist the urge to use this time to be on your smartphone. When your child sees you on your phone, it sends the signal that you are unavailable.

- If you observe a neighbor, friend, or even celebrity doing something that impresses you or might resonate with your child, point it out. This modeling behavior is important for your child to observe. It gives him someone to look up to and may help shape how he behaves in the future.

- If you walk past a homeless person on the street, use it as an opportunity to make an empathic comment to your child. Although homelessness can be difficult to talk about, this gives you a chance to make a nonjudgmental observation about different experiences people have.

- As you walk through the park, a way to develop your child's observational skills is to point out the big and little things: a flower that you otherwise may not have noticed as well as a towering tree that lots of kids are climbing.

- Look through a magnifying glass with your child. Ask her to observe how things look different when looking through it. This can help her focus on details.

What Kids Can Do:

- If you hear someone speaking a language you don't recognize, ask what it is.

- When you try a new food, keep it in your mouth a little longer than usual to observe how it feels and tastes.

- If you're outside and see a flower, smell it.

- When you walk into a room, make it a game. How many things of the same color are in that room? What does the floor look like? Is there a rug? Is anything hanging on the walls? You can practice becoming a careful observer.

Story 1 Hannah has Alopecia Areata, a skin disease that results in baldness. Bald from the time she was one year old, people wrongly assumed her baldness was a result of cancer treatment. She feels empathy for kids who are, in fact, receiving treatment for cancer and wanted to do something to cheer them up. When she was ten, Hannah had the idea to make pretty headbands and ball caps for boys and girls who were receiving treatment in a nearby children's hospital. As word spread, people within and beyond Hannah's town offered to help. Children and adults donated money, supplies, and time. Realizing how much support there was for her idea, Hannah began a charity to reach children in other areas of the country. To find out more, visit www.bowsandballcaps.com.

A BOW OR BALL CAP MAY MAKE THEM REALLY HAPPY

WHEN THEY HAVE NO HAIR.

—Hannah Grubbs, founder of Bows and Ballcaps

Story 2 Lots of people visit homeless shelters but not everyone is moved to action the way that Sarah was. When she was seven years old, she visited a homeless shelter with her brother to deliver a donation of sleeping bags. While she was there, the manager told her that they really needed socks. "I decided to donate socks. My first idea was to bring a basket to my class but then more people heard about my campaign." Sarah's first donation was thirty-nine pairs of socks. Over the following ten years, Sarah donated 2,400 pairs of socks and raised $85,000.

I HOPE TO ALWAYS GIVE WHEREVER I AM.

IT'S NOT A PLACE, IT'S THE DOING THAT MATTERS.

—Sarah Lewis, founder of Socks Warm Your Heart

⟶ Questioning

> Life's most persistent and urgent question is,
> "What are you doing for others?"
>
> —*Dr. Martin Luther King, Jr.*

For You to Read:

Questioning things that you see as unfair can lead in many different directions. Questioning may help you understand why things are the way they are. Questioning may contribute to a feeling of compassion for people in a situation different from your own. Questioning can challenge previously held beliefs. Questioning can lead you to reflect on ways you, in particular, can make an impact. And questioning can lead you to investigate ways to make changes.

We give a great gift to our children when we encourage them to learn to question things that don't seem right. Help them find answers rather than giving them answers. This process keeps them involved and teaches them to problem-solve, one step at a time.

To Read with Your Child:

Asking questions can be very powerful. It shows that you're paying attention to what is going on and are interested in finding an answer. If you don't understand something or are confused, ask a question. If you see something that does not seem fair to you, question it. If you don't know how to help, ask "What can I do?"

What Parents Can Do:

- If your child feels something isn't okay and doesn't have the words to articulate it you can help. Try offering a few ideas to see if you can put their feelings into words.

- If you notice that there have been a lot of soda bottles and cans in the trash can at your local park, ask yourself what you can do. You might start a petition with your friends and neighbors requesting that the town put recycling bins in the park.

- When you see a person who is blind standing at the corner, ask if you can help them cross the street.

- Think about how many things have been impacted by just one person asking a question. Recount to your child a time in history when someone asked a simple question that led to real change.

What Kids Can Do:

- If there is something you're interested in that you want to learn more about, ask your teacher. For example, if you like animals, ask your teacher if the class can take a field trip to the zoo.

- The next time your mom or dad is reading a book to you and you don't understand what one of the words means, ask.

- When you see a friend crying or looking sad, ask, "What's wrong?"

- If you see someone at school eating something you never saw before, ask, "What are you eating?"

- If you see a dog walking without a person, and you think it might be lost, ask your parents how you might help.

Real-LIFE
Story 1

Five-year-old Phoebe felt sad when she saw a homeless man begging for food. When it was time for each child in her day care center to do a community service project, she decided to help feed people who are hungry. She chose to collect and recycle soda cans with a goal to raise $1,000 for the San Francisco Food Bank, which was her local food pantry. Phoebe's teacher was encouraging but careful to point out that this was a really big goal. Phoebe wrote letters to family, friends, and neighbors asking for their help in donating soda cans. Word spread about Phoebe's project and people donated not only soda cans, but also money. Phoebe surprised everyone. She not only collected and redeemed the cans, she counted the money and wrote thank-you notes to people who contributed to her project. Phoebe raised $3,736.30, which translated into 17,800 hot meals!

> WE COLLECT CANS AT HOME.
> WHY CAN'T WE DO IT FOR THE FOOD BANK?
>
> —*Phoebe*

 Kayleigh's dad is a police detective. Although he is not part of a "K9" team, sometimes he needs to work with dogs and trains with them. Kayleigh loved to watch her dad train the dogs and took pictures of them. When making an album of those photos, she noticed that only some of the dogs wore bulletproof (ballistic) vests. When Kayleigh asked why all of the dogs did not have protective vests, she was told that many police departments could not afford to buy them. Each dog vest cost more than $600! Although Kayleigh was only six years old, she decided to raise the money needed for a dog vest. Since then she has donated vests to K9 teams in Maryland, Virginia, California, and North Carolina.

> I SELL MY TOYS BECAUSE I WANT TO HELP THE POLICE DOGS.
> I AM SELLING LOTS OF STUFFED ANIMALS AND STUFF AT HOME...
> MY STROLLER, BIKES...THREE BIKES.
>
> —*Kayleigh Crimmins, founder of Kids for K9s, Inc.*

⫸ (be) Yourself

> WE ARE ALL, EACH AND EVERY ONE, UNIQUE IN THE UNIVERSE.
> AND THAT UNIQUENESS IS WHAT MAKES US VALUABLE.
>
> —*James A. Owen, author, illustrator*

For You to Read:

Remind your child that there is no one else just like him or her. Every person can offer something unique to the world—something different from anyone else. Each of us has our own way of being in the world that we can share for good. As adults, we can help children feel pride in their particular strengths or talents, which can result in positive feelings about who they are. Children who feel better about themselves are more likely to give of themselves. Teaching children to appreciate their uniqueness, and supporting it yourself, will improve their self-esteem and ultimately help them be more engaged in their world.

To Read with Your Child:

There is only one you! Think of yourself as "you-nique." You have the power to accomplish great things. Take time to think and talk about what you can do with your family, school, or community. Just as you have your own unique fingerprint you can make a "you-nique" difference in the world around you.

- Everybody's unique. What are ways your sister (or brother or best friend) is unique?
- Pick three words from the following list (or think of your own) that you would like other people to use when they describe you. Why did you choose those words?

Adventurous	Happy
Artistic	Hard-working
Athletic	Helpful
Brave	Honest
Calm	Loving
Chatty	Nice
Cheerful	Quiet
Creative	Sensitive
Energetic	Serious
Friendly	Smart
Funny	Strong
Generous	Talented
Gentle	Thoughtful

What Parents Can Do:

- Help your child realize how he or she is unique. When your child does something in a way that reflects his or her individuality, point it out.
- If you're cooking with your son and he arranges the food in a special way, tell him a lot of kids wouldn't take the time to do what he did.
- When your daughter notices that the guinea pig's water bottle is empty and refills it, remark that she takes good care of her pet.

What Kids Can Do:

- Look back at the three words you chose to describe yourself. How can you use those qualities to be kind to people?
- If you picked "cheerful" or "funny" to describe yourself, maybe

you could cheer someone up when they are upset. You can talk to them, sing to them, or just sit with them.

- If you picked "energetic," "hard-working," or "athletic," you can help clear the table or carry in grocery bags without being asked.

Maria Keller loved to read. She was shocked when her mother told her that not all children have books. "I was amazed that so many kids in the world don't have books and I wanted to fix that," she said. When she was eight she began collecting books through her church and soon discovered that many people were interested in helping her. Maria set a goal to collect one million books by the time she turned eighteen and she began a charity called Read Indeed to make this happen. At thirteen, she collected her millionth book—five years early! Describing her experience when giving a child a book, Maria said: "It is amazing to see the looks on their faces when you hand them a book." Maria's new goal is to distribute books to children in all fifty states and every country in the world by her eighteenth birthday. To find out more, visit www.readindeed.org.

Lilly has a rare genetic disorder called Usher Syndrome that affects her vision and hearing. When she was in second grade, she and her family started to raise money for the Foundation Fighting Blindness, which is devoted to developing treatments and cures for eye diseases like the one affecting her. Lilly is slowly losing her vision and hearing but that has not stopped her from doing everything she can to help other people who are also suffering from vision and hearing loss. Lilly and her family participate in walk-a-thons and other fundraisers. To date they have raised over $150,000 for the Foundation!

I HOPE FOR A FUTURE FILLED WITH SIGHT,

SOMETHING YOU MAY TAKE FOR GRANTED. EACH DAY

I STRUGGLE WITH READING, SCHOOLWORK, EVEN OPENING MY

LOCKER COMBINATION, LET ALONE RUNNING ON THE SOCCER FIELD,

BUT I AM DETERMINED NOT TO LET THIS GET ME DOWN.

I KNOW THAT EVEN I CAN MAKE A DIFFERENCE. I AM DETERMINED

TO RAISE MONEY FOR RESEARCH BECAUSE I KNOW . . .

KNOW IT WILL MAKE A DIFFERENCE.

—Lillian Diuble

Part Three

Taking It Further

Approaching Tough Conversations

Children need to learn about different aspects of life. Who better to teach them than you? How many times have you tried to have a "difficult" conversation with your child but gave up because you did not know how to begin, were uninformed, caught off guard, or just not comfortable with the topic? It is okay not to have a conversation at the moment your child raises something. Let her know that you will talk to her and need a little time to think about her question so you can answer her thoughtfully. You may need to make an "appointment" to return to the conversation later in the day or the following day, choosing a time and place to initiate the conversation so it goes as smoothly as possible. That way, you can listen carefully to your children and give them the attention that they need to know that you take them seriously and that their concerns are important to you. Dr. Sara Konrath, a prominent social psychologist, studies empathy development in children. One of the factors she sites as important is parents' willingness to talk about their child's emotions and how their child's behavior affects others.[1] You can educate yourself in preparation for a conversation. Part of that process may be exploring your attitudes about the topic. And remember, as always, your opinions will be conveyed through your words and body language. Before you answer a tough question, you may want to assess what your child already knows. Just ask. It can be challenging to talk about people who are homeless, abandoned animals, children with illnesses, terrorism, and other topics that kids are curious about. Don't let that deter you. To make it easier, here are some conversation starters for situations that frequently arise. You know your child best; think about other topics that you anticipate he or she might bring up and create your own conversation starters. You might want to use the Journal Pages at the end of the book to write your thoughts about those topics. These challenging conversations can be an opportunity to teach your child what the kind or compassionate thing to do would be in a difficult situation. You never know where these conversations or kindnesses will lead.

Your child is staring at someone.

Your instinct may be to say, "Stop staring!" Instead, start talking. Curiosity is normal. We all look at each other, especially when someone looks different from us. It's not *that* you look; it's the message you send *with* your look. Clearly, you won't be able to have this conversation in the moment. However, as soon as you and your child are alone, ask him how he would feel if someone were staring at him and then quickly looked away. What if someone were looking at him, and smiled when she caught his eye? He probably would have a different reaction in that case, and that is what you're trying to teach him. The kind thing to do would be to smile and even say hello, creating a momentary connection.

Your child's friend has two daddies.

"Why does Liza have two daddies?" asks your child. Let your child know that all families are different. Although it may be new or confusing for your child to see a family constellation different from your own, such as one with two gay dads, the message you can share is that families are about love. Regardless of who the "parents" are (it might be just one parent, two daddies, two mommies, grandparents, aunts, or uncles) as in your family, they love each other and they love their children.

Your child sees a commercial for animals that have been abused and need to be adopted.

Your child asks, "Why can't we adopt some of these dogs and cats?" While appreciating how big your child's heart is you can explain that it is not practical for your family to take in a large number of animals.

However, it is important to respond to your child's desire to help. Research and discuss what you *can* do. Your child might collect towels, raise money to donate dog food, or arrange a time to play with the cats and dogs at a shelter. You might even consider financially supporting an animal at a shelter. And, of course, you can discuss, as a family, if actually adopting a pet is a good idea!

Your child asks how come some nights Annie stays at her mom's and other nights at her dad's?

Regardless of your youngster's age, you do not need to say a lot. Give a simple, factual explanation using words your child understands. Annie's parents are divorced, which means that they are no longer married to each other so now they no longer live together. Even if you know details, it is inappropriate to share specifics about the couple's life and relationship with your child. You may wish to say that even though the parents decided that they needed to live apart they will always love their children. At the end of this conversation, or a few days or weeks later, your child may have more questions. One of which may be, "Are you going to get a divorce, too?" You can tell him that you love your spouse and do not plan to get a divorce. Most of the time, particularly for a first conversation about divorce, it is just the basic information and reassurance that a child needs.

Your five-year-old child comes home asking what it means to be adopted after hearing her friend say that she is.

Every child has birth parents but not all children are raised by them. There are different reasons why birth parents may not be able to raise their children. You don't need to elaborate on those reasons unless your child asks. And if you do give examples, try not to be judgmental about another person's circumstances. Tell your child that children who are raised by different parents than the ones who gave birth to them are "adopted." The parents who are raising them are their adoptive parents. Adoptive parents love their children, take care of them, make their favorite dinner, and cuddle when they're reading stories. They do everything other parents do except give birth to their children.

You and your child walk past someone pushing a shopping cart filled with belongings and a sleeping bag.

"Why is that person pushing a shopping cart full of stuff?" your child asks, clearly confused. You might want to use this as an opportunity to start a conversation about homelessness by saying that it makes you feel sad to see someone who doesn't have a home. Your child seems worried that this person has neither a place to go nor a family to take care of them. Validate the concern and let him know that in your community there are resources available to provide coats, places to shower, and safe places to sleep for people who are homeless. If your child continues to talk about it or appears to want to help, you might research organizations in your area that provide services to people who are homeless. There might be a way your family can volunteer or engage with one of them.

A child in your neighborhood is ill.

Your child was looking forward to seeing a neighborhood friend and doesn't understand why now they can't play in the snow together. You know that this friend is living with a chronic illness and is at a higher risk if he gets wet and cold. Sensing your child's disappointment, you realize this may be the time to share more detailed information. You know your child best, convey enough information to help him understand why his friend can't be outside. Remind your child that they can still have their playdate, it just has to be inside. Frustrated, your child says he doesn't want to go anymore. Ask him how he thinks his friend might feel having to deal with this kind of disappointment and change of plans regularly because of his health and the weather. You can use your child's reaction as a way to teach empathy for his friend's situation.

Your child comes home from school talking about a lockdown drill.

Your child comes home visibly shaken after experiencing the first lockdown drill of the year. "Why do we need to do something like this? It was really scary hiding under the desk." Tell your child that it is important for the students and teachers to practice so they know what to do if something bad happens. Listen carefully to your child's fears and address them. If you don't already know, ask your child's school what the students are told before a drill like this so you have the same information and are using language consistent with what they're hearing at school. You might also talk to your child about calming strategies to practice when he is upset or during the next drill.

Your nephew is visiting and talks about being bullied.

During a family get together, your twelve-year-old nephew tells you and your child about being bullied in the park and how someone he didn't know helped him. Listen compassionately as he tells his story. Give your child a chance to speak and ask his cousin questions if he has any. Then, ask your child what might have happened if this bystander had not come to his cousin's aid. Focus on the important role that bystanders play. If this person had not observed what was going on and been willing to get involved, your nephew might have been hurt and the bullies would have won. You can discuss what the person who helped might have been thinking or feeling when he chose to step in. Acknowledge to your child that this is a difficult, but important and brave thing to do. Remind your child that there may be times when he can't do anything. If that is the case, he should try to find an adult who can.

Your four-year-old child asks, "Where do babies come from?"

You can ask her where she thinks they come from to get an idea what she believes or knows already. Start simply when you answer. You may find that a brief response, such as, "They grow in a place in the woman's tummy called a womb (or uterus)" may be enough information for your child. If your child asks how the baby got there you can tell her that, "The sperm (or seed) from the man and an egg from the woman came together." This is probably as much as, if not more than, a four-year-old will want or need to know. This may be your first conversation about sex but you don't want it to be your last. Some very young children get information from older kids—their siblings, friends' siblings, older kids on the school bus—but you want to be the one to give her accurate information. When your child does want more information or asks how the man's seed got there, use the example that is appropriate to your family. For instance: it might be that the daddy put his penis into the mommy's vagina; or that the embryo or growing baby grew in another woman's tummy; or it might be that a doctor helped put the seed in the woman's tummy. Whatever you say, it is helpful to be as relaxed and comfortable as you can be. This will convey to your child the underlying message "I can ask my parents anything." You want your kids to be able to come to you with any questions they have about their bodies, sex, or whatever is on their minds. Your responsiveness sends the message that you respect their curiosity and are open to talk about and think through any topic they bring up.

When you're in the supermarket you help someone in a wheelchair reach something from a high shelf.

As you and your child are grocery shopping you come upon a woman in a wheelchair who is struggling to reach a box of cereal on a high shelf. You ask if you can get it for her. As you and your child continue shopping, your child says, "Look at how many things that lady won't be able to reach." Let your child know that he is very observant and sensitive for noticing the limitations when someone is in a wheelchair. This might start a conversation about the daily challenges and adaptations that someone faces when they're in a wheelchair. You can also share with your child that having a wheelchair gives the person using it independence and opportunities that she would not otherwise have. When you leave the supermarket, point out a curb cut that makes it easier for people in wheelchairs or pushing strollers to navigate crosswalks. These observations will help your child develop empathy and understanding for people whose daily life challenges may be different from his own.

A person asks you for money for food. You decide to give a sandwich.

Your child asks, "Why aren't you giving the man money since that's what he asked for?" You explain that you are more comfortable giving food than money to someone you do not know. You and your child tell the man you're happy to buy him a sandwich and ask what kind he would like. After you give the man the sandwich and have walked away, you may wish to take the conversation further and add that sometimes people spend money that they get for food on other things like drugs or alcohol. By buying the food, you're helping in a way that is comfortable for you and you're sure that he is getting something to eat.

After an illness your family's eleven-year-old pet cat died and you have to tell your five-year-old child.

Since this is likely the first time your child is confronting death and loss, here are a few suggestions. As with all of these tough conversations, be honest. Tell your child that, as he knows, the cat was sick and her body could no longer function so she died. Share your own sadness at this loss and let your child express how he feels about the loss of his beloved cat. Children have a variety of emotions and responses to death. Some, especially younger children believe it is temporary or may not believe you. Some children may cry, others may appear angry, and others may have little visible reaction. However your child reacts to this loss is okay. If he asks specific questions about what happened or what will happen to the cat now, answer simply and honestly. A child's bond with a pet is unique. Some may not realize how connected a child and animal can be and we want to be conscious to honor that special relationship. If you are burying the cat, let your child know when that is happening and ask if he wants to be there. If you're not, it is still important that your child has closure. An important part of the grieving process is time. During that time, you can encourage your child to actively remember and memorialize their dear pet. You might ask your child if he wants to write a letter, draw a picture, print photos of himself and the cat, or anything else that resonates. Don't be shy to talk about the joy you and your family felt from your cat even if it makes you sad.

After a hurricane that impacted your neighborhood, your child is having trouble sleeping.

Although your family was safe, your community was impacted by a recent hurricane. You lost power for several days and couldn't get around easily due to fallen trees and power lines. Your child knows people who suffered greater losses and needed to relocate to a shelter temporarily. Your child has had trouble sleeping and been clingier than usual since the storm. As you talk to your child about what happened, acknowledge how scary it was. Remember that these feelings can last far longer than the duration of the event. Point out everything the first responders in your community did during the crisis and how well they handled the situation. Even though this was a really hard experience to go through, focus on how strangers helped one another and the whole neighborhood came together. Reassure her that she and your family are safe now, and give her practical tools to help her feel more relaxed. (For some ideas look at Chapter 6.) Talk to your child about any ideas she has for how to be best prepared if something like this happens again. If she can't come up with any, remind her that you bought bottled water, batteries, and extra food to help your family be as comfortable as possible during and after the storm.

A parent in your child's class dies.

You receive notification from the school that a parent in your child's class died unexpectedly. How do you tell your child? Pick a time and place that are appropriate for this conversation. Think about where your child might be most comfortable for this difficult conversation. For some kids, holding their teddy bear or petting the dog will make them feel at ease. For other kids it will be taking a walk with you or sitting on your lap in their favorite chair. Start by letting your child know that you have upsetting information to share with her. Be honest, being sure to convey only age appropriate information. While it is reasonable to express your feelings, be mindful of not overwhelming your child with your own sadness or surprise. You want her to feel safe and have room to express her own feelings or ask questions. Different children will have different reactions. It's okay if she doesn't initially appear to be very upset; it may take time for her to process the information or she may not be as affected by the news as you anticipated. She may have lots of questions or not want to talk further. As a follow-up conversation, you might talk with her about what to say the first time she sees her friend.

Your child heard about "good touch" and "bad touch" as part of a training program at school.

Although childhood sexual abuse prevention may not be something that any of us want to talk about, this is one of those conversations that has to happen. From a very early age, children can feel empowered about their bodies. They intuitively know what is appropriate and inappropriate and need to be encouraged to pay attention to their "inner voice." We need to give them information to prevent ambiguous or dangerous situations and the tools to say NO when something bad is happening. Nobody should be looking at or touching their body in a way that makes them uneasy. Conversely, children should never be asked to touch someone else's body if they don't want to or are uncomfortable doing so. Your children may be confused when they go for their checkup and the doctor wants to look at or touch their private parts. Let them know that if you are in the room too, it is okay because the doctor is making sure that they are healthy. Tell your children that it is not okay if anyone (whether they know them or not) touches them and tells them to keep it a secret. And if they find themselves in that situation, they need to tell you or another adult. You can use this conversation to differentiate a good secret (like a surprise party or a birthday gift) from a harmful secret. And even though it may seem innocuous to you, respect their wish if they do not want to give a relative or friend a hug or kiss. By doing this you are encouraging them to maintain control of their body.

Finding Formal Experiences

You and your family may be ready to introduce something more formal and organized into your kindness practice. Chances are this will involve visiting or volunteering at a particular program or organization. In this chapter we will help you focus on the type of experience you're looking for and the best way to go about finding a good match. We will also share ideas about how to make the experience as successful as possible, many of which come from young people who are deeply involved in their volunteer projects. Use the questions below to get you thinking about your past experiences and your current volunteer interests.

THE MOST POWERFUL EXAMPLE A CHILD IS
AFFORDED IS THE CONDUCT OF A PARENT OR GRANDPARENT.
THE CHILD WATCHES AND EMULATES HOW THEY INTERACT
IN THE WORLD, HOW THEY TREAT OTHERS, WHAT PRIORITY THEY
GIVE OTHERS, AND WHAT LANGUAGE THEY USE TO DESCRIBE OTHERS.
PARENTS AND GRANDPARENTS ARE LIKE THE SOIL FROM WHICH
A PLANT PULLS ITS NUTRIENTS: THEY CAN OFFER A RICH ENVIRONMENT
THAT ENCOURAGES THE CHILD TO LIVE WITH GRATITUDE AND
LOVE OR A BARREN BACKDROP WHICH PRODUCES A
CHILD BEREFT OF EMPATHY OR MERCY.

—Susan Sparks,
pastor, Madison Baptist Church, NYC

Read through and think about the questions below. When you are ready to write down your responses, this questionnaire, and room to write your answers, are in the Journal Pages at the end of the book.

Questionnaire

What volunteer experience, if any, did you have as a child?

Was that experience your idea or did someone else initiate it?

Did you go alone or with friends or family?

Was the experience organized through a particular group (religious institution, school)?

Looking back, do you think the experience was age appropriate? Did it reflect your interests?

How did this volunteer experience affect you?

What volunteer experiences did you have as a teenager and have you had as an adult?

If you did volunteer, was it because you cared about a particular cause, because it was the "right" thing to do, or because it was what your friends were doing?

If you didn't volunteer, why didn't you?

Are you currently volunteering? Is your volunteer experience satisfying to you? Why or why not?

As a parent interested in bringing volunteerism to your family, think about how your family spends free time.

How much time do you want to commit to a volunteer opportunity?

One time for a few hours

At holidays

Two or three times per year

On a monthly basis

On a weekly basis

What population or topic interests your child and family?

Animals

Children

Chronically Ill

Civics

Domestic Violence

Elderly

Environment

Homeless

Hungry

LGBTQ

Mentally Ill

Physically Disabled

Refugees

Veterans

Other _____

What type of setting interests you?

Day Care Program

Hospital

Library

Park

Physical Rehabilitation Facility

Religious Organization

Senior Center

Shelter

Soup Kitchen

Zoo

Other _____

What setting, if any, would you not be comfortable visiting?

Do you have an understanding as to why you are reluctant to go to a particular setting?

What do you want your child to get out of a volunteer experience?

Which of your child's strengths would you like to encourage in a volunteer experience?

Would you prefer a volunteer experience to be just members of your own family?

Would you be open to including another family or your children's friends?

Find a Good Match

Now that you have had a chance to hone in on what you're looking for in a volunteer experience for your family, you can help your child find a good match. Through that match, he can create meaningful connections with others. Build on successful "one time" experiences he may have had. If he was excited about a program that brought animals from the local nature center into his school, try to visit that center. This could be a good place for your child to volunteer or help in some way. Perhaps a recent religious school visit to a local senior center will develop into an interest in regularly visiting senior residents in your community.

> THE GROUP OF PEOPLE THAT WE ENDED UP
> WITH WAS JUST THIS GROUP OF PEOPLE THAT I DON'T THINK,
> IF YOU PUT US IN A HIGH SCHOOL TOGETHER, WE WOULDN'T HAVE
> BEEN FRIENDS BUT THROUGH THE PROCESS OF WRITING WE
> FORMED THIS REALLY STRONG, UNEXPECTED COMMUNITY.
>
> —*Talia Young,*
> *Looking for Home (Spoken Word Workshops)*

If you're starting from scratch, let the questionnaire guide you as you look for a good match. Involve your children in the search. The goal is for them to be as invested as possible since research shows that people who put more effort into their kind acts experience greater well-being.[1] For instance, if your child is interested in animals or the environment, you might start by doing a preliminary search—through your town or online. To prevent your child from becoming overwhelmed, once you have a list of possible options, narrow it down and review them together. You might want to look at the website for each organization with your child so the two of you can better understand what each one does. Additionally, there are several organizations that evaluate the efficiency with which charities spend the dollars they bring in. Three such examples are: Charity Navigator, GuideStar, and CharityWatch. Encourage your child to ask questions then look for the answers together. For younger children, have a few prepared in advance in case they don't have any of their own. Your questions will probably encourage them to generate their own. It is important for older children to understand how the organization works by asking questions like:

What is their mission?

Who runs the organization?

Who or what need do they serve?

How long have they been operating?

Where do they get most of their money from?

How do they spend their money?

How well are they rated by an organization that monitors charities?

How many volunteers do they have?

What do their volunteers typically do?

You and your child may want to use the Journal Pages at the back of this book to write down some of the answers you find because you may be comparing different organizations.

The first place you call or visit might not be a good match. That is okay. Keep looking. It's more important to find the right match than to rush into an inappropriate one. You know your child better than anyone. For some children, the consistency of going to the same place and doing the same thing repeatedly is comfortable and rewarding. Other children may need the novelty of doing lots of different things—maybe at the same place or maybe having different experiences in a variety of settings. You'll know the type of environment in which your child will thrive—follow your instincts.

Of course with very young children we, as their parents, are guiding their actions. Part of the motivation for starting young is to teach children a love of and appreciation for kindness and helping others. They will internalize this desire and become motivated to seek out these opportunities independently as they get older. This is referred to as autonomous motivation. And research shows that autonomous motivation improves the experience for both the giver and the receiver.[2]

> I GOT INVOLVED IN MY PROJECT BECAUSE
> WHEN I WAS FIVE YEARS OLD, MY MOTHER BROUGHT
> ME TO A HOMELESS SHELTER SO I COULD SEE HOW OTHER
> PEOPLE WERE LIVING AND I COULD BE MORE
> APPRECIATIVE OF EVERYTHING I HAVE.
>
> —*Nicholas Lowinger, Gotta Have Sole*

Be Prepared

Once you have found the right match, you might consider taking a personal or virtual tour or talking to someone who has volunteered there before your child begins. Help your child answer the questions that follow or other basic questions before beginning the volunteer experience. This will help your child get off to a smooth start. There is space for you to write your answers in the Journal Pages at the end of the book.

What does the place where they are volunteering look like?

What will they do?

How much time will they spend volunteering?

Who will they work with?

Will they know anybody?

How many people will they see when they go to volunteer?

Tell your child what about this particular experience you think is a good match for their strengths.

Another aspect of being prepared is thinking about both the positive and negative emotional impact these experiences can have. Encourage your child to be aware of feelings that may come up throughout their experience. Parents play an important role in teaching children the language they don't yet have to describe their feelings. Children as young as three years old can identify emotions, but the ability to name them isn't fully formed until they're about six years old.[3] It is equally important to help your child name feelings such as satisfaction, pride, or joy as it is frustration, apprehension, or worry that can result from your child's engagement. These early conversations about feelings between you and your child can create a habit of talking about emotions, which is not always easy. Model for your child the importance of taking care of yourself so you have the emotional, mental, spiritual, and physical reserves to draw on when you are interacting with others. While your child's volunteer experience may not be as intense as an adult's experience, it can certainly affect him. We have relaxation and mindfulness exercises in Chapter 6, which can help children relax and take care of themselves as they engage with others.

COMMUNITY SERVICE IS SO IMPORTANT
BECAUSE YOU GET TO SEE FIRSTHAND HOW MUCH OF
A DIFFERENCE YOU CAN MAKE. DOING COMMUNITY SERVICE
ALSO ALLOWS YOU TO BECOME MORE GRATEFUL FOR WHAT YOU HAVE.
I DIDN'T REALIZE THE IMPACT THAT CELEBRATE U WOULD
HAVE ON OUR VOLUNTEERS. I AM ALWAYS THRILLED TO
SEE THE SMILING FACES OF THE CHILDREN WE CELEBRATE
AND I AM JUST AS EXCITED TO SEE THE JOY OUR
PARTIES BRING TO THE VOLUNTEERS.

—Talia Eskenazy,
Celebrate U

Make It Meaningful

Another opportunity for a meaningful conversation is after you've
visited the place where your child will volunteer. Encourage your child
to represent her experience in some concrete way such as using photos,
a collage, drawing, storytelling, or a model. This representation makes
what your child is doing come alive and reinforces different aspects
of her experience. It will also give you insight into what she got out of
the visit.

THE WORLD IS NOT ABOUT "ME, MYSELF AND I."
IN ORDER TO LIVE A RICH AND MEANINGFUL LIFE, CHARITY
AND THINKING OF OTHERS AND HELPING IS A HUGE COMPONENT.
ONE CAN LEARN SO MUCH BY HELPING OTHERS
AND THE REWARDS ARE TREMENDOUS.

—Yumi Kuwana, philanthropist
and founder of Global Citizens Initiative

We can help our children understand the multiple ways what they are doing benefits them as well as others. There are many ways to be kind. Doing so helps kids develop confidence and they learn from a very young age that they can make a difference in the world. They can share what they know, learn new skills, and in the process, even have fun. If your child sings or plays a song at a senior center, and talks about how the residents participated by joining in or clapping, discuss how hearing that familiar tune reminded residents of another time in their life. Explain how that memory likely triggered feelings of joy they felt another time they heard that song. You may find this is a gateway to a deeper conversation with your child. Allow it to unfold. Remember the details your child shares so you can refer to them in the future (Here's another chance to use those Journal Pages!). You may discover something you did not know about your child when you ask her how this experience made her feel.

> EVERYBODY CAN DO THEIR PART TO REPAIR
> THE WORLD AND IT DOESN'T HAVE TO BE A GIANT GESTURE.
> FINDING SOMETHING THAT YOU'RE PASSIONATE ABOUT
> AND USING THAT TO MAKE A CHANGE. IF EVERYBODY IS
> TRYING TO MAKE A LITTLE CHANGE, THEN, TRULY,
> YOU CAN MAKE A DIFFERENCE IN THIS WORLD.
>
> —*Skylar Dorosin, Project 2020*

Include the Whole Family

With everyone's busy schedules it can be hard to carve out time to volunteer. Try reconsidering the way you spend your free time as a family to see where a volunteer experience can best fit into your life. You may volunteer once or twice a year, monthly, weekly, or even daily. Some families volunteer while on vacation. You may bring needed supplies to the area you're visiting or spend one or two days of your trip in service. There are lots of opportunities available to willing families.

For most families volunteering together reinforces the values they want to live by and many parents say that they feel like they are leaving a legacy by doing so.[4] Families often describe feeling closer, more like a team, and fulfilled when they share a volunteer experience together. When working toward a shared goal, everyone in the family brings something unique to accomplishing the task at hand. In this new setting, you may see different sides of people you know well. A family volunteer experience is also a great way to disconnect from technology and connect with each other creating experiences and memories that become part of your family history.

Decide, with your children, what you would most enjoy doing. If they are a part of the decision, they will likely feel more connected and committed. And when they feel that commitment, you may be less likely to hear complaints about getting up early, driving a distance to volunteer, or other such challenges that can be associated with finding the right venue for your whole family. When referring to volunteering with their parents, "Children mention appreciating and respecting them more and seeing how much they care for the community."[5]

I WOULD ENCOURAGE FAMILIES TO CREATE A
CULTURE OF GIVING TO FIND OPPORTUNITIES TO SERVE TOGETHER.
IT HELPS TO GET TO KNOW THE ORGANIZATION AND TO
FIND WAYS OF INVOLVING EACH GENERATION IN THE PROCESS.
GIVING TO OTHERS TOGETHER HELPS EACH FAMILY MEMBER

TO FOCUS ON SOMETHING BIGGER THAN HIM OR HERSELF,

WHICH KEEPS LIFE IN PERSPECTIVE FOR ALL OF US.

—Rev. Dr. Heather Wright,
director of Greenwich Center for Hope & Renewal

You may not "officially" volunteer every day but you can certainly make kindness part of your everyday life, especially within your family. Think about simple ways to increase kind behavior. You might compliment someone in the family on the delicious meal he made, do a magic trick to cheer someone up when she is sad, offer to help with someone else's chores, or play an extra game of catch with the dog. These everyday acts of kindness can help strengthen your family's bond.

The Importance of Relaxation: Tools for Breathing, Visualization, and Meditation

Whether starting a new project, visiting an unfamiliar place, or man-aging the ups and downs of daily life, kids may feel some anxiety. That is to be expected. Breathing, meditation, visualization, and other relaxation exercises are useful, easy to teach tools that can both help children manage their feelings and be more connected to themselves and to the world around them. Studies of children who regularly practice these techniques strongly support their effectiveness.[1] These children show a heightened compassion for themselves and others, improved focus, increased resilience and self-esteem, and a sense of inner calm. It is never too early to start. Providing our children with these tools, which will change and grow with them, gives them a way to remain in control of their thoughts and emotions in both challenging and everyday situations. While you may have read about or have firsthand experience with the positive impact of these tools with adults, you may not have realized that children do great with them, too. Whether you are experienced or a novice, practicing relaxation with your child is a lovely thing to do to have special time together.

Think about the variety of ways that people you know respond when they feel uncomfortable, apprehensive, or worried.

Have you seen someone use tools that you appreciated because they were particularly helpful?

Now, think about how you respond when you feel uncomfortable, apprehensive, or worried.

Is what you typically do helpful? Why or why not?

What do you usually tell your child to do when they feel uncomfortable, apprehensive, or worried?

Is that helpful? Why or why not?

Have you ever tried any relaxation exercises?

Does anyone you know practice them?

You and your family may feel that you're always rushing or hardly have time to catch your breath. In this chapter we provide a selection of simple scripts for parents to help children relax and feel more comfortable in a variety of situations. Try them to see which fit best for you and your family. Doing these exercises with your child, even for a few minutes, will give you the chance to relax together. You'll notice that some of the scripts teach breathing, some teach progressive muscle relaxation, and others teach guided meditation or visualization. Different people prefer different strategies so try them all with your child. You may find that one helps your child in the morning and another before bed. We hope you'll share our commitment to the importance of incorporating these techniques into your child's life. Bringing our full attention to the present moment can make a significant difference in the way we experience the world. If you decide that you would like to explore further, or find that none of the scripts below resonate with you and your child, there are CDs and Apps that we have found useful listed in the Resources section.

There are many ways you can introduce the idea of practicing relaxation exercises to your child. One way you might start is by encouraging your child to take a few deep breaths as part of his bedtime routine. This will help him wind down from the day and prepare for sleep. It will also help him get used to the feeling of calm inside. You may prefer to start by reading a picture book on the topic of mindfulness or relaxation, talking about your own experience with one of these techniques, or discussing a time when he felt very uncomfortable or worried and it wasn't handled as well as he might have liked. If your child has already been exposed to some of these tools in school or has a friend who told him about their experience, you can build on that. The goal is to help your child understand that by regularly doing one or more of these brief exercises he can call on them as needed to help him feel calm.

Eventually, anywhere and at any time, your child will be able to draw on these techniques. To start, however, it is important for you to help your child create a routine. Try to pick a similar time each day or every other day to practice. Find a relatively quiet, comfortable place where your child can focus and won't be interrupted. This could be their bed, a chair on your porch, or a particular corner of a room in your home. Use a quiet, soothing tone of voice as you slowly read the scripts to your child. This along with a comfortable setting will help create an environment for relaxation. You may want to encourage your child to do the same script more than once before deciding if it feels right for them. Dr. Richard Davidson and other experts in this field remind us that doing a regular practice of breathing or looking at something "mindfully" increases our depth of relaxation and our ability to concentrate. They liken this practice to strengthening a muscle. So, you will want to tell your child (and remind yourself) that like learning anything new this takes practice. It can take a while; don't give up!

Scripts

Below are several scripts for you to experiment with as you and your child explore the basics of mindful observation, breathing, relaxation, and guided visualization. You can start with just three to five minutes every day, every other day, or every few days with very young children and five to ten minutes with older children, depending on how they take to the practice. You may wish to start and finish the exercise with a bell or a chime sound. You can set a timer on your phone for a specific amount of time. These exercises can help a child keep their mind focused rather than racing. Remember, each child is different and will have his or her own experience. Use these scripts as a starting point. Feel free to adjust or personalize them in the way that works best for your child. Try not to judge through a lens of success or failure. Just have the time together.

Brief breathing meditation for children of all ages:

Sit and feel your body on the chair.

Place your feet flat on the floor.

Place your hands in your lap or on your legs.

Close your eyes if that is comfortable for you.

Relax your shoulders.

Slowly, breathe in.

Slowly, breathe out.

Feel the air come into your nose.

Feel the air go out of your nose or mouth.

Do it again.

Inhale and exhale slowly.

Focus on your breath.

When your mind starts to wander, think about your breath.

Slowly, breathe in.

Slowly, breathe out.

Feel the air come into your nose.

Feel the air go out of your nose or mouth.

Begin to feel calm.

One more time.

Breathe in.

Breathe out.

Feel your body relax.

Belly breath meditation for children of all ages:

You can also focus on your breath by picturing the air coming deep into your belly. This is called a "belly breath" and helps us to relax and stay focused on our breath. Sit on a chair or lie down on the bed or the floor. Relax your body. Put one hand on your belly. Picture a balloon in your belly. Try to imagine it clearly. What color is it? As you inhale, picture the breath moving all the way into your belly, blowing up the balloon. As it inflates, what happens to the color of the balloon? Breathe in and feel your belly rise under your hand. As you breathe out picture the balloon deflating and feel your belly go flat under your hand. As you breathe into your belly it will help you feel calm. When your mind wanders, bring it back by paying attention to your breathing and picture your balloon inflating and deflating with your breath.

Just a few of these calming breaths help us to focus.

Mindful Exercises for the Senses— for Children of All Ages

Mindful looking

Start by looking closely at the palm of your hand. Just look. Notice the color and shape. Does the color change from finger to finger? Is the skin crinkly? Smooth? Is your skin shiny? Dull? Look at how long your fingers are. Which one is the longest? Which is the shortest? Now look at your thumb. Is it pointing in a different direction from the others? Does it move differently from your other fingers? Watch your fingers when you wiggle and stretch them. Now look at the lines in your palm. Are they long or short? Deep or shallow? Which area of your hand is puffy? Look carefully. We see things differently when we take time to look carefully. That is when we notice things.

If you are able to really concentrate on the details of your hand, you will find you are looking at your hand and not thinking about anything else. You are in the present moment. You also may be breathing more slowly than you were before you started to focus in this way.

Thoughts for parents:

Once your child has looked at her hand in this way, ask her if she noticed something new. Your child can practice this by looking closely at something else: a flower, an orange, a chair, their fish—there are infinite possibilities. This helps her notice what she might not have seen at first. You can continue to encourage your child to raise her awareness about the world around her by being interested in what she brings to your attention. Even when you are in a rush, if your child points out something she notices, take a breath and spend a minute to share what she has seen.

Mindful touching and tasting:

Try putting something into your mouth (a berry, a spoonful of peanut butter) and feel it on your tongue and the roof of your mouth. Maybe it rolls behind your teeth or inside of your cheek. Pay attention to the shape, the texture, the size, and the taste. Notice the difference when you bite into it. Is it squishy? Sticky? Hard? Bumpy? Smooth? Can you feel the seeds? Is the skin rough? Is the inside of the berry juicy? Pay attention and slowly experience what is happening inside of your mouth. You may want to close your eyes so you can concentrate better.

If you are able to really concentrate on the details of the food in your mouth, you will find you are focusing on what it feels and tastes like and not thinking about anything else. You are in the present moment. You may also be breathing more slowly than you were before you started to focus on the taste and texture in this way.

Thoughts for parents:

Once your child has felt and tasted the food in this way, ask him if he noticed something new. Your child can practice this by touching and tasting something else: ice cream, a vegetable, cake; don't limit him. This helps him notice what he might not have felt or tasted at first.

Mindful listening:

Sit or walk in a quiet place. Listen. Allow yourself to hear the small sounds that you may not have heard before. Pay attention to the hum of an air conditioner, the buzz of a refrigerator, the chirping of birds, or listen to your own breath. Just be aware of how many sounds there actually are when we think there is silence.

If you are able to really concentrate on the sounds that you normally do not hear or pay attention to, you will discover you are focused on listening and not thinking about anything else. You are in the present moment. You also may be breathing more slowly than you were before you started to focus on listening carefully.

Thoughts for parents:

Once your child has listened in this way, ask her if she heard something new. Your child can practice this by listening closely to some other sounds: a specific piece of music, a conversation, "city sounds," "nature sounds," and notice what she might not have heard at first. Attending to sounds that we often miss can be a particularly illuminating activity in a world with what seems to be an ever present background of buzzes, rings, beeps, and pings.

Mindful smelling:

(For younger children you may want to adjust the vocabulary.)

Before you drink or eat something, smell it. Inhale the aroma and be aware of the smell of something you may eat or drink every day. You may never have noticed how this food smelled until this moment. Or maybe by paying attention, you become aware of several different scents that are mixed together. This experience may trigger a memory or a connection that you were unaware of. Just notice it and breathe in.

If you are able to really concentrate on the details of an aroma, you will find you are focused on the smell or fragrance and not thinking about anything else. You are in the present moment. You also may be breathing more slowly than you were before you started to focus on smells in this way.

Thoughts for parents:

Once your child has inhaled a particular scent in this way, ask him if he noticed something new. Your child can practice this by intently smelling something else: a flower (or a bouquet of flowers), herbs, food as it cooks, fresh produce, shampoo, and notice what he might not have smelled at first.

Progressive muscle relaxation script

Introduction for parents:

In 1908, Dr. Edmund Jacobson, a physiologist and scientist at Harvard, began his work with relaxation training. He is considered the founder of progressive muscle relaxation training techniques that are widely used with children and adolescents. He believed that you could remove muscle tension throughout the body by tensing and relaxing specific muscle groups. This method, called Progressive Muscle Relaxation (PMR), teaches an ordered way to go through your body tensing then relaxing muscle groups while paying attention to the sensation associated with each state. Practicing this exercise will teach your child to be aware of where they hold tension in their body and how to release it. Read the script aloud to your child as they learn this technique. As with all of the other scripts, remember to read slowly using a quiet tone of voice. Take your time—it is not a good idea to rush through relaxation! Once your child becomes adept at using PMR, they can practice it on their own. The ultimate goal is for them to have confidence that they can use this exercise, or a small part of it, at any time they need to relax their body. The great thing is that nobody will know if they are "squeezing a lemon" or actively relaxing.

There are several ways to "progress" through the body for relaxation. We think A.S. Koeppen's progressive muscle relaxation training script for children, published in 1974, is still one of the best.[2] It incorporates some fun visualization to help children relax, particularly at the end of the day or when they feel stressed.

It is important to read this text as it is. The purpose of this exercise is for your child to learn how to move through their body, tensing and relaxing each muscle group. Of course, if your child is afraid of elephants, feel free to replace the elephant with a bear or a more reassuring animal, but keep the structure of the script intact so they get the full benefit. Find a quiet and cozy place. Some children will prefer to do this exercise seated in a chair while others will prefer to be lying down. Both work equally well. Use pillows and blankets if your child would like them to get more comfortable. Turn off or dim the lights. With a quiet and gentle voice, guide your child with these directions:

Script

By relaxing our body we can relax our mind to feel calm. We can even get rid of butterflies in our stomach! Let's do these relaxation exercises together. As we do them, pay attention to how your muscles feel when they are tight and also when they are relaxed. (If your child is in a chair, suggest that they sit back, get both feet on the floor or put them out straight (uncrossed), and just let their arms hang loose. If they are in bed, suggest they lie on their back and feel the mattress underneath their body.) *Okay. Take a deep breath and let it out slowly. Now take another deep breath and do the same. Close your eyes and don't open them until I tell you to. Listen carefully to my words and try to pay attention to what you feel in your body.*

Hands and Arms

Make believe you are holding a lemon in both of your hands. Now squeeze the lemon, really hard, as if you are squeezing all of the juice out of the lemon. Now, notice how tight your hands and your arms feel as you do this. Now, open your hands and drop the lemons. Notice how different your hands and arms feel when they are relaxed. Good. Now imagine that

you are taking two more lemons and squeeze them even harder than the
first time. Good; real hard. Now drop the lemons and relax. Pay attention
to how much better your hands and arms feel when they are relaxed. You
may even notice a warm or tingling feeling in your fingers. (If you prefer,
you can focus on one hand and arm at a time.)

Arms and Shoulders

Imagine that you are a dog or a cat. Stretch your arms way out in
front of you. Lift them up high over your head. Stretch them way back.
Feel your shoulders get tight. Stretch higher and feel a pull in your arms
and your shoulder. Now drop your arms down to your sides. Okay, puppy
or kitty, let's stretch again. Stretch your arms out in front of you. Raise
them over your head. Pull them back, way back. Pull hard. Now let them
drop quickly. Good. Pay attention to your shoulders and how much more
relaxed they feel. Let's do it again, and this time, when your arms are
above your head, reach up so high that you try to touch the ceiling (or the
sky if you are outside). *Stretch your arms way out in front of you. Raise*
them way up high over your head. Push them way, way back. Notice the
tension and pull in your arms and shoulders. Hold tight, now. Great. Let
them drop quickly and notice that good, relaxed feeling.

Jaw

Imagine you have a hard piece of gum in your mouth and you need to
soften it up. Now bite hard to soften it. Feel the stretch in your neck and
your jaw. Let your neck muscles help you. Now relax; let your jaw hang
loose. Notice how good it feels just to let your jaw drop. Okay, try it again.

Bite down hard and move your jaw so your teeth in the top of your mouth slide on the teeth in the bottom of your mouth. Bite hard! Now relax again. Just let your jaw drop. Notice the difference in your mouth.

Face and Nose

Imagine that a fly has landed on your nose. Without using your hands, try to get him off your nose. Good for you. Wrinkle up your nose. Make as many wrinkles in your nose as you can. Scrunch your nose up real hard. Good. That bug flew away. Now you can relax your nose. Watch out, here comes the bug again. Wrinkle up your nose again. Shoo him off. Wrinkle it up hard. Hold it just as tight as you can. Good work, he flew away. You can relax your face. Notice that when you scrunch up your nose your whole face scrunches up, too! Your cheeks and mouth and your forehead and even your eyes get tight. So, when you relax your nose, your whole face relaxes, too, and that feels good. Now you can relax. Let your face become smooth, no wrinkles anywhere. Your face feels nice and smooth and relaxed.

Stomach

Hey! Here comes a cute baby elephant. But he's not watching where he's going. He doesn't see you lying in the grass, and he's about to step on your stomach. Don't move. You don't have time to get out of the way. Just get ready for him. Make your stomach very hard. Tighten up your stomach muscles real tight. Hold it. It looks like he is going the other way. You can relax now. Let your stomach go soft. Let it be as relaxed as you can. That feels so much better. Oops, he's coming this way again. Get ready. Tighten up your stomach. Real hard. If he steps on you when your stomach is hard, it won't hurt. Make your stomach into a rock. Okay, he's moving away again. You can relax now. Settle down, get comfortable, and relax. Notice the difference between a tight stomach and a relaxed one. That's how we want to feel—nice and loose and relaxed. You won't believe this, but now the elephant is coming your way again and not turning around. He's headed straight for you. Tighten up your stomach muscles. Make them really hard. Here he comes. This is really it. You've got to hold on tight. He's stepping on you. He's stepped over you. Now he's gone for good. You can relax completely. You're okay now and you can feel nice and relaxed.

This time imagine that you want to squeeze through a narrow fence and the boards have splinters on them. You'll have to make yourself very skinny if you're going to make it through. Suck your stomach in. Try to squeeze it up against your backbone. Try to be skinny as you can. You've got to be skinny now. Now relax and feel your stomach being warm and loose. Okay, let's try to get through that fence now. Squeeze up your stomach. Make it touch your backbone. Get it real small and tight. Get it as skinny as you can. Hold tight, now. You've got to squeeze through. You got through that narrow little fence and no splinters! You can relax now. Settle back and let your stomach come back out where it belongs. You can feel really good now. You've done fine.

Legs and Feet

Now pretend that you are standing barefoot in a big, fat mud puddle. Squish your toes down deep into the mud. Try to get your feet down to the bottom of the mud puddle. You'll probably need your legs to help you push. Push down, spread your toes apart, feel the mud squish up between your toes. Now step out of the mud puddle. Relax your feet. Let your toes go loose and feel how nice it feels to be relaxed. Back into the mud puddle. Squish your toes down. Let your leg muscles help push your feet down. Push your feet. Hard. Try to squeeze that puddle dry. Okay. Come back out now. Relax your feet, relax your legs, relax your toes. It feels so good to be relaxed. No tenseness anywhere. You feel kind of warm and tingly.

Conclusion

Stay as relaxed as you can. Let your whole body go limp and feel all your muscles relaxed. In a few minutes I will ask you to open your eyes. As you go through the day, remember how good it feels to be relaxed. Sometimes you have to make yourself tighter before you can be relaxed, just as we did. Practice these exercises every day to get more and more relaxed. A good time to practice is at night, after you have gone to bed and the lights are out and you won't be disturbed. It will help you get to sleep. Then, when you are really a good relaxer, you can help yourself relax at school or wherever you are. Just remember the dog or the cat or the elephant, or the bug or the gum, or the mud puddle, and you can do your exercises and nobody will know.

Today is a good day, and you are ready to feel very relaxed. You've worked hard and it feels good to work hard. Very slowly, now, open your eyes and wiggle your muscles around a little. Very good. You've done a good job. You're going to be a super relaxer.

Loving-Kindness Meditation Script for Children of All Ages

Loving-Kindness meditation "is the practice of directing positive thoughts and well wishes to ourselves and others."[3] It is referred to as "Metta" or compassion meditation in the Buddhist tradition.

This simple practice is easy to teach children. It can be particularly helpful for children who show deep concern for others they encounter through their volunteering or anyone who is in need. Children may feel that they are actively helping others by practicing this Loving-Kindness meditation because of the simple repetition. In this abbreviated version, as you will see in the script, your child will first focus on him- or herself, then on a close family member or the whole family, followed by a friend. Then, his or her focus will be direct to others (people or animals) about whom he or she is concerned. Finally, the focus returns to him- or herself.

Script:

Loving-Kindness Meditation for Kids (adapted from Lauren Chaitoff)[4]

> *Begin by saying and sending yourself the following Loving-Kindness meditation:*
> *May I Be Happy. May I Be Healthy. May I Be Safe.*
> *Repeat this to yourself two or three times until you can really feel it inside your heart.*
>
> *Now, think about someone you love and picture this person in your mind. As you see this person in your mind, send them the Loving-Kindness meditation.*

*May **You** Be Happy. May **You** Be Healthy. May **You** Be Safe.*
Repeat two or three times.

Now, think about someone you like a lot and picture them in your mind. Think about this person and send them the Loving-Kindness meditation.
*May **You** Be Happy. May **You** Be Healthy. May **You** Be Safe.*
Repeat two or three times.

Next, think about a person you do not know too well, yet see often. It can be a neighbor, a teacher in a different class or a person who works in the cafeteria at your school. Think about this person and send them the Loving-Kindness meditation:
*May **You** Be Happy. May **You** Be Healthy. May **You** Be Safe*
Repeat two or three times.

Now think about people or animals who need help or extra care and send them the Loving-Kindness meditation:
*May **You** be Happy. May **You** Be Healthy. May **You** Be Safe.*
Repeat two or three times.

Now think about someone who bothers you and who can get on your nerves. Send this person the Loving-Kindness meditation:
*May **You** Be Happy. May **You** Be Healthy. May **You** Be Safe.*

Take this Loving-Kindness meditation and make it even bigger by sending it out to the entire world.
*May **We All** Be Happy. May **We All** Be Healthy. May **We All** Be Safe.*
Send it out to the entire country!

Finally, come back to yourself.
*May **I** Be Happy. May **I** Be Healthy. May **I** Be Safe.*

Guided Imagery Script— for Children of All Ages

Introduction for parents:

Guided imagery is a way to tap into your imagination to help you become relaxed. Using this method, we paint a picture in our mind. We draw on the strong "mind-body" connection as we incorporate our senses, which will allow us to experience this picture as real. We can create any image and be anywhere. The idea is to close our eyes and "visit" that place. Once we are in this imaginary place, we want to be aware of our surroundings. We focus our attention on what we see, feel, hear, and smell as we notice an increased feeling of relaxation and comfort. The beach is one popular image to induce relaxation (listening to the sounds of waves and shorebirds, feeling the sensation of sand between our toes, and noticing the breeze on our skin).

You can offer an image to your child or ask him to tell you about a place that he likes, where he felt calm and safe. If you and your child are creating a "script" together, ask your child to describe the place he is thinking of in detail. What does he see, hear, and smell there? Maybe it is a special bench in the park, or a rock he has sat on looking at a lake in the woods, or a garden, or even a cozy chair at his grandparents' house. Or, because you know your child well, rather than "going to a specific place," he may like the image of having a soft, golden cloak around him, or maybe if he is outdoors, you can guide him through the exercise of breathing in the light of the sun and exhaling it to others. You can use our script as a model or create one on your own or with your child.

Script:

Find a place where you can feel very comfortable.

Take a deep breath in and let it out slowly.

When you are ready, close your eyes. Imagine that you are on the beach.

Notice the color of the water and whether the waves are big or small.

Can you see the tiny birds along the shore? Notice the seagulls flying in the sky.

Feel the wet sand in between your toes.

Watch the waves.

Feel the sunshine and a slight breeze on your body.

You feel relaxed and happy.

Remember how you feel. This is the feeling of your very special place. You can relax in this place. Say to yourself: "I am relaxed, my body feels warm and good. I am happy and safe here."

Enjoy the feeling of deep relaxation.

When you are ready, slowly open your eyes and stretch your arms and legs. Breathe in a long and deep breath and then let that breath out slowly.

You are now back in this moment, feeling relaxed.

Guided Imagery Script about Volunteering for Children 8 and Older

Sit comfortably in a quiet place.

Close your eyes if you are comfortable doing so.

Be aware of the sounds and the smells around you.

Slowly breathe in as you count, 1, 2, 3.

Slowly breathe out as you count 1, 2, 3.

Continue breathing like this.

Feel the breath going deep into your belly.

Create a "picture" in your mind of what you would like to see if you could change something that disturbs you in the world (examples of what you might picture are hungry children eating healthy food; trash in a vacant lot being replaced with plants and flowers; empty shelves in a hospital playroom filled with books and toys).

Focus on the details of your picture.

Relax your body and breathe as you focus on your "picture."

Breathe in and out as you count, 1, 2, 3.

Sit quietly.

Imagine different ways to make that picture become real.

When you are ready, breathe and focus on your picture again.

Open your eyes.

Write down or share your ideas with someone.

As you can see, there are many ways to approach relaxation with your child. We hope at least one of the above scripts resonated with you and if not, that you will continue to explore different techniques until you find one that does. The benefits to your child may be immediately obvious in how she handles challenging or upsetting situations. Or, you may find that these exercises are creating a foundation for her to feel more relaxed in general when going through her daily life or approaching a new situation. Either way, we hope you will see what the research supports: Kids benefit.

7

Troubleshooting

IF YOU'RE TRYING TO ACHIEVE, THERE WILL BE ROADBLOCKS.

I'VE HAD THEM; EVERYBODY HAS HAD THEM.

BUT OBSTACLES DON'T HAVE TO STOP YOU.

IF YOU RUN INTO A WALL, DON'T TURN AROUND AND GIVE UP.

FIGURE OUT HOW TO CLIMB IT, GO THROUGH IT,

OR WORK AROUND IT.

—*Michael Jordan, basketball player*

Life has its challenges no matter what age you are. In this chapter, we will help you and your child address some of them. It takes time to become comfortable with new experiences and there are always surprises. That's to be expected. You know your child best. Is your child easily thrown by a change of plan or is your child typically able to go with the flow? If you notice reluctance or discomfort that concerns you, there are probably particular factors contributing to your child's reaction. Engage your child to try to find out what they are. Remember that these hiccups can be opportunities for you to teach your child how to navigate the unexpected.

Roadblock:

You see your child being unkind.

Your child may:

Be afraid of the other child—Find out why.

Be part of a larger group that is teasing or being unkind to another child—Remind your child that although you know it is hard to stand up to other kids, what they were doing was unkind and not okay.

Not like the other child—Let her know that regardless, it is not the right thing to intentionally say or do something mean or hurtful to another child.

Think that the other child was unkind to them or a friend—Encourage your child to ask an adult to intervene. Or, if that isn't possible, tell your child it's okay to walk away if necessary.

Blame someone else for their own frustration or disappointment—Unkind words or actions may be an easier way for your child to express their disappointment. Point this out.

Not be aware that what they're doing or saying is unkind—Ask her how she would feel if someone had done or said the same thing to her.

Example: Eight-year-old Samantha was on the sidelines after her soccer game when her mom heard her say to a teammate, "I can't believe you missed that shot. You made us lose the game." Although she felt the urge to intervene in the moment, her mom resisted. On the way home after the game, she started a conversation with Samantha, "I overheard what you said and I was very disappointed." Samantha responded, "But it was her fault that we lost!" Her mom reminded her that although the last shot did influence the outcome of the game, so did the way everyone else on the team played before that shot. Samantha's behavior was unkind, unsupportive, and did not show good sportsmanship. Rather than address all of these issues, Samantha's mom had to decide which one to focus on. She chose to discuss how unkind Samantha's comment was to her teammate. Her mom asked, "How would you feel if you were the one who missed that last shot? What would you have wanted to hear from your teammates?"

Example: Jake, six years old, ate his snack in the car as his mom drove him home from Little League practice. When he finished his pretzels, Jake threw the empty bag out of the window. Surprised, his mom stopped the car and very calmly said, "We don't do that. We will talk about it when we get home." When they got home, Jake ran to play outside but his mother had a different idea. She suggested a "trash walk" (that's when you walk around the neighborhood picking up trash). As they walked with a bag, his mom asked, "Hey Jake, what would happen to all of this garbage if we were not picking it up today?" Jake thought and said, "I don't know. I guess it would just sit here." Jake made the connection that he has a responsibility to do something to keep the neighborhood clean.

Tips for navigating the roadblock:

Have patience. Don't talk about something with your child when you're feeling overly emotional—wait. This way, you'll have time to think about what you want to say and how you want to say it. Too often we respond impulsively, risking overdoing it, and/or missing a valuable opportunity for discussion.

Even if your child does something "wrong," avoid having a solely punitive response. You may have told your child to be kind to others or that you don't drop trash, but the message has not yet been heard or internalized. Because change takes time, you may need to share this message many times in different situations before it sinks in. These moms created teachable moments by showing their children how hurtful being unkind—both to other people and the environment—can be.

Roadblock:

You think your child is ready for a "life lesson" but your timing is off.

Your child may:

Be insufficiently prepared—Just because you have been thinking about and preparing to share your idea for days doesn't mean your child is prepared. You have to get him ready to hear the lesson. Think about how you can break it down into smaller parts.

Not be developmentally ready—In some ways your child may seem old beyond their years. However, there are lessons that kids can't learn until they're physically, cognitively, and emotionally ready.

Be preoccupied—Something may have happened earlier in the day that is still on your child's mind. If that is the case, your child will likely be thinking about that and less open to what you want to teach him. Assess your child's mood. Context and timing are vital when presenting an idea to a child.

Be distracted—You will need your child's attention to help him focus on the lesson you want to share. You know your child best. If he is talkative and open to conversation when he is drawing, that may be a good time to start. If your child gets totally engrossed in building with Legos and doesn't like to be interrupted, think about a different time to start the conversation.

Example: After his friends left his birthday party, four-year-old Andrew was playing with his new toys. His mom thought this would be a great time to introduce the concept of sharing with those who don't have as much. "You got so many new toys," she said, "let's pick three of them to give to children who don't have any." Confused, Andrew began to cry and shouted, "No, they are mine!" In her frustration his mom said, "You have so much. Don't be selfish." Although wanting to teach him to be generous with others, the message was lost because her emotions got in the way and the timing was wrong. Developmentally, Andrew cannot understand why his mother wants him to part with what he just got. He didn't even have a chance to enjoy his new toys when he was expected to give some away.

Tips for navigating the roadblock:

Even when you are upset with your child's response, pay attention to yours. This mom was disappointed and labeled her son "selfish" when he wanted to hold onto his toys. She knew she wanted to convey the value of sharing with those in need. What she did not realize was that she had to actually teach him this idea. If you are critical and judgmental it will be much harder for your child to absorb what you want him to learn. Preparing him in advance probably would have made this little guy more receptive to the important lesson this mom was trying to teach.

Perhaps the outcome would have been different if, before Andrew's birthday, his mom had prepared him by saying, "You are going to get lots of new toys at your party. After you open your gifts, I will help you go through the toys you already have in your room and you can pick three to give to children who don't get toys on their birthdays."

Roadblock:

One of the ways you want to teach your child about kindness is through volunteering. Your child says she wants to do it but behaves as if she doesn't.

Your child may:

Be afraid—Find out what she is afraid of. Perhaps she is afraid of meeting new people in a new place. Remind her that you'll be with her.

Not know what to expect—Describe where she will be and what specifically she will do. Use photos, a website, take a tour, or talk with other people who have done similar things or have volunteered at the same organization.

Be worried she "can't do it"—Assure her that she will learn what she needs to know and won't be expected to do it until she's ready. As with anything, the more she does it, the more comfortable she will feel.

Be unsure of what to say—Help her practice by role-playing conversations for different situations.

Want to go with a friend—Think about which of her friends would be well suited to this experience and suggest those children.

Be uncomfortable about being with people she perceives as very different from herself—Acknowledge her concerns; it's normal to have them. One of the fun things about volunteering is learning from people who are different from us. Emphasizing the ways they are similar may help put her at ease.

Have difficulty making a choice because of the number and variety of opportunities available to her—Narrow the options that you initially present. Start with a particular focus—helping homebound elderly, animals, or the ocean environment. Maybe the activity is visiting a neighbor every week, playing with stray animals at the local shelter, or picking up trash from a nearby beach or riverbank.

Not want to sacrifice her playtime—Make sure there is enough time. Play is a vital part of a child's developmental process.

Example: Kim's mother was always interested in helping the elderly. This became her passion over many years of volunteering at an assisted living facility. She eagerly looked forward to the time when her daughter would accompany her on these visits. When Kim was five years old, she went on a short visit to meet some of the residents her mom had come to know and love. Kim was quiet and clingy. Surprised, her mother assumed that with more exposure, Kim would become more comfortable. When it was time for their second visit, Kim became noticeably upset and said she did not want to go. Instead of talking to Kim about it, her mom proceeded as planned. The second visit proved no better than the first. After a third unsuccessful visit, this mom realized that her daughter was too unhappy to continue.

Tips for navigating the roadblock:

Simply put, one size does not fit all. The fact that you enjoy doing something does not necessarily mean that, by extension, your child will. This may be disappointing. Kim's mom may have noticed but not wanted to acknowledge some of the factors that contributed to her daughter's discomfort. Our children will learn to express their feelings when they know that we will listen and work with them. It's not always easy to recognize what our child's concerns and feelings are, but it is important to try. Sometimes we exhibit our emotions with our bodies. This gives a clue to how we are feeling. When you sense from your child's body language that she is uncomfortable, afraid, or hesitant, describe how you think she may be feeling. Tell her you are making this guess based on her "body language." You are teaching her that feelings can be communicated through physical behavior. When children learn to pay attention to these physical cues they will become more aware of how they feel.

Being aware of physical cues will also help them become sensitive to how others feel. This is a valuable skill for developing empathy. Although the assisted living facility still may not be a good match for Kim, she and her mother would have had practice talking about what contributed to Kim's reluctance, which might have been helpful.

Roadblock:

The "perfect" project is not such a good match anymore.

Your child may:

Have lost enthusiasm, become bored with, or lost interest in the project—Is this about the setting, the project or the result of something personal? Ask your child what might help him get reconnected. If he can't come up with an answer, offer some suggestions.

Be expected to do what is no longer age appropriate—Find out if there is a more age appropriate responsibility or task available. If not, perhaps you and your child can work to create one.

Want to do more or something else but it isn't possible in the setting—Follow your child's lead, as he may now be ready for a different experience. Explore other options with him.

No longer see the impact of what he's doing—Take this opportunity to discuss with him the concrete ways he has made a difference.

No longer have time for the necessary commitment—Find out if he can maintain his connection while investing less time.

Feel discouraged that what he's doing is not enough—
Ask why he's feeling this way. Acknowledge that his
observation is accurate and it can be discouraging knowing
how many people are in need. Help him focus on the impact
he is having.

Feel overwhelmed—What is this about? Maybe this is just a busy
week—for him or at his volunteer location. Take a step back
and help him evaluate if this is unusual or the new normal.

Just need a break—Then take one. Volunteering shouldn't feel like
a burden. Let him go back when he is ready. A break may be a
necessary step in preserving his commitment in the future.

Example: Since he was little, Sean and his father have been donating
to the local food pantry. When they do their grocery shopping,
they buy an extra can or box of food to add to their collection bag
at home. When the bag is full, Sean's dad drops it off at the pantry.
Now seven years old, Sean told his dad, "It's kind of boring just
putting food in the bag." His dad understood that Sean was ready
to do more but wanted to make sure he appreciated the impact of
what he had already done. "Think about how many bags we fill up
every year. All that food goes to people who cannot afford to buy it
for themselves. I can see why you are bored, though. Now you are
old enough to do more. Any ideas?" In response to Sean expressing a desire to meet some of the people who were getting the food,
his dad suggested they deliver the food together and see if they can
help distribute it to the people who use the food pantry. They also
agreed to volunteer to serve at the Thanksgiving dinner hosted by
the food pantry.

Tips for navigating the roadblock:

Help your child see how what he has done has helped other people even if it is not obvious to him. This can help him see the value in his effort, which he may not see anymore. Additionally, by asking, "How does it make you feel when we do this?" you have the opportunity to talk with him about how he has benefited from what he is doing. If he cannot come up with an answer, show him what you mean. You might say, "I feel good knowing that someone is not hungry because of the food we collected."

Now that we've uncovered some of the roadblocks that your child may encounter, let's explore some that are more relevant to you. You may have more influence over your child when he is younger but your interests may be in conflict when he is older. Think about how you might manage that situation.

Roadblock:

My child wants to volunteer with a particular population or in a particular setting that makes me uncomfortable.

You may:

Be unaware of the power of your language and actions—Be conscious of how you express yourself to your child and others. Your attitudes become apparent through what you say and do in your everyday life. For example, you may avoid talking to or clearly be uncomfortable with someone who has an obvious impairment.

Need to examine your own attitudes—Recognize that your own
attitudes influence the way you direct or respond to your child's
interests. Some of our attitudes are so deeply ingrained that
we are unaware of them and the possible biases they represent.
Self-examination will help you, and, by extension, your child,
become more comfortable.

Avoid unfamiliar situations or be reluctant—Take risks. Explore
new situations that may take you out of your comfort zone. Let
your child open new possibilities for you. Your child's interest in people who are homeless may give you the opportunity
to become engaged with people whom you have previously
avoided.

Example: Stephanie's church is sponsoring a holiday project for the
Sunday School children where they will visit an inner city shelter
bringing holiday gifts and food for the residents. Although she
wants her children to do "good works," she has never been there,
and is afraid of the neighborhood where the shelter is located.

After presenting the idea to her nine-year-old son who sensed her
reluctance he said, "It doesn't sound like you want me to go." Stephanie was confused by his response. But when she thought about it, she
became aware that it may have been her body language that communicated her discomfort. Until her son said something, she was unaware of
how obvious her concerns were. "Thanks for telling me. I probably feel
this way because I don't know the neighborhood. Sometimes we judge
places that are unfamiliar and I am afraid that is what I did. I think it
will be a great experience for you and I want you to go with the church
group. I am going to find out more so that I get more comfortable."

Tips for navigating the roadblock:

It is important for Stephanie to acknowledge and verbalize her self-awareness because her son may have ascribed a different meaning to her concern. For example, he may have wondered whether it was safe to be with children who lived in a shelter, a question that is based on his mother's fear rather than fact. If you do have a concern, share with your child a reasonable explanation for why you feel hesitant. Think about what it will take to work through your fear so you don't transmit it to your child. Of course, you want to be more at ease with what your child is doing both for your own comfort and so you can support his effort. Perhaps you get more information from the church or talk to other parents whose children have visited this shelter in the past. You might ask to chaperone the trip to share the experience with your child. Or, you might want to think about other ways to reduce your worry. You might go back to Chapter 6 for some ideas.

 **Conclusion**

UNLESS SOMEONE LIKE YOU CARES A WHOLE AWFUL LOT,
NOTHING IS GOING TO GET BETTER. IT'S NOT.

—*Dr. Seuss, author*

We hope that reading *The Kindness Advantage* **has given you and** your child a variety of ideas for incorporating kindness into your family's daily life. As is the case with many books for parents of young children, this book is very much about the foundation and fundamentals. From this starting point, your family can build on the fundamentals of kindness in the way that works best for your child's age and interests. Revisit *The Kindness Advantage* again in a year or two. See how far your family has gone with the fundamentals. Who knows? You might find ideas that work well for you in the future that might not resonate with you now.

By practicing kindness at home (as a quick refresher that would include paying attention, showing patience, communicating respectfully, and showing compassion and concern for others), we both model kindness and help our children lay the foundation for kind and compassionate interactions outside of our home. These may include everyday encounters with family, friends, neighbors, and even strangers as well as more "formal" situations such as in volunteer settings. All of these interactions will impact the way your child thinks about the larger world.

119

The research we discussed in Chapter 1 makes a strong case for starting early. Take advantage of the countless opportunities to reinforce the fundamentals of kindness. We often notice and highlight our children's athletic, musical, artistic, and academic achievements from an early age with the hope of encouraging those skills. Make the same effort to take note of their "achievements" when they show compassion and caring for others. When we acknowledge our child's considerate thoughts and actions, we reinforce the essential value of kindness. And the more often we engage in acts of kindness, the happier we will feel. As leaders in the field of compassion tell us, we are wired for it. Our role as parents is to nurture that natural inclination toward kindness and compassion in our children.

To develop compassion and empathy we need to be able to see the challenges in the world and find ways to talk about and address them. The Real-Life Stories provide a window for you and your child to gain insight into other peoples' experiences—both those who are struggling with particular challenges and those trying to help ameliorate those challenges. We hope that the tips we provided for approaching tough conversations were useful. Of course, those are just a few examples of conversations that come up fairly often. There will always be awkward moments and difficult conversations. Stick with it—with practice you will gain confidence in your ability to navigate dialogue on these tough topics.

Taken together, the fundamentals of kindness: acceptance, commitment, connection, empathy, giving, interest, nurturing, observing, questioning, and be(ing) yourself, along with the tips and tools in this book, can start your child on the path to a meaningful life of caring for others. We hope we have inspired you to believe that, with *The Kindness Advantage*, your child can be a force for good and change in the world.

Recommended Reading

STORYTELLING IS ONE OF THE STRONGEST TOOLS
WE HUMANS HAVE WHEN IT COMES TO CULTIVATING EMPATHY
AND UNDERSTANDING DIFFICULT SITUATIONS AND THOSE
DIFFERENT FROM US. STORIES ALLOW A READER OR LISTENER
TO MOMENTARILY ENTER THE CHARACTER'S MIND AND
UNDERSTAND THEIR SITUATION AS OUR OWN.
IT IS THE KEY TO CULTIVATING KINDNESS.

—Lisa Bubert, librarian, storyteller, writer,
Using Books to Build Kindness blogpost Library.Nashville.org

These are some of our favorite books that we have loved reading to
our children and grandchildren as they have grown. Some are picture
books for little ones, others are about real life kids and teens that you can
read aloud or give to an older child. Each book conveys elements of *The
Kindness Advantage* through its story and characters. Books are a great
way to expose your child to something or someone new in an organic
way. Whether you are reading to your child or suggesting a title for an
older child to read independently, a book can be a wonderful starting
point for a conversation about kindness. This is yet another way of inte-
grating *The Kindness Advantage* into your child and family's daily life.

THERE ARE MANY LITTLE WAYS TO ENLARGE
YOUR CHILD'S WORLD.
LOVE OF BOOKS IS THE BEST OF ALL.

—Jackie Kennedy

Recommended Picture Books:

26 Big Things Small Hands Do by Coleen Paratore (Free Spirit, 2008)

A Chair for My Mother by Vera B. Williams (Greenwillow Books; Reprint Edition, 2007)

A Handful of Quiet: Happiness in Four Pebbles by Thich Nhat Hanh (Plum Blossom Press, 2012)

A Very Big Bunny by Marisabina Russo (Schwartz and Wade, 2010)

Abigale the Whale by Davide Cali (Little, Brown Books for Young Readers, 2006)

Alexander and the Terrible, Horrible, No Good, Very Bad Day by Judith Viorst (Atheneum Books for Young Readers; Reprint Edition, 1987)

An Invisible Thread Christmas: A True Story Based on the #1 New York Times Bestseller by Laura Schroff (Little Simon, 2015)

Be Kind by Pat Zietlow Miller (Roaring Brook Press, 2018)

Be Who You Are by Todd Parr (Little Brown Books for Young Readers, 2016)

Brave Irene by William Steig (Square Fish; Reprint Edition, 2011)

Children Just Like Me (Dorling Kindersley, 1995)

Dad, Jackie, and Me by Myron Uhlberg (Peachtree Publishers, 2010)

Each Kindness by Jacqueline Woodson (Nancy Paulson Books, 2012)

Frog and Toad Are Friends by Arnold Lobel (HarperCollins, 2003)

George and Martha One Fine Day by James Marshall (HMH Books for Young Readers, 1982)

Hair for Mama by Kelly A. Tinkham (Dial Books, 2007)

Happy Birthday, Moon by Frank Asch (Alladin; Reissue Edition, 2014)

Heart Bubbles: Exploring Compassion with Kids by Heather Krantz, MD (Herow Press, 2017)

Hope for Haiti by Jesse Joshua Watson (G.P. Putnam's Sons, 2010)

I Am Ghandi (Ordinary People Change the World) by Brad Meltzer and Christopher Eliopoulos (Dial Books, 2017)

I Am Helen Keller (Ordinary People Change the World) by Brad Meltzer and Christopher Eliopoulos (Dial Books, 2015)

I Am Jackie Robinson (Ordinary People Change the World) by Brad Meltzer and Christopher Eliopoulos (Dial Books, 2015)

I Am Rosa Parks (Ordinary People Change the World) by Brad Meltzer and Christopher Eliopoulos (Dial Books, 2014)

It's Okay To Be Different by Todd Parr (Little Brown Books for Young Readers; Reprint Edition, 2009)

Mind Bubbles: Exploring Mindfulness with Kids by Heather Krantz, MD (Herow Press, 2017)

Miss Rumphius by Barbara Cooney (Puffin Books, 1985)

Moody Cow Learns Compassion by Kerry Lee MacLean (Wisdom Publications, 2012)

Moody Cow Meditates by Kerry Lee MacLean (Wisdom Publications, 2009)

Mrs. Katz and Tush by Patricia Polacco (Dragonfly Books; Reprint Edition, 1994)

My Most Favorite Thing by Nicola Moon, Carol Thompson (Dutton Juvenile, 2001)

My New Best Friend by Sara Marlowe, Ivette Salom (Wisdom Publications, 2016)

One Green Apple by Eve Bunting (Clarion Books, 2006)

One Love by Cedella Marley (San Francisco: Chronicle Books, 2011)

Puppy Mind by Andrew Jordan Nance (Plum Blossom Press, 2016)

Reach Out and Give by Cheri J. Meiners (Free Spirit, 2006)

Ruff by Jane Hissey (Random House Books for Young Readers, 1994)

Sheila Rae the Brave by Kevin Henkes (Greenwillow Books, 1996)

Sitting Still Like a Frog: Mindfulness Exercises for Kids by Eline Snel and Myla Kabat-Zinn (Shambhala; Pap/Com Edition, 2013)

Starbright: Meditations for Children by Maureen Garth (HarperOne, 1991)

Somebody Loves You, Mr. Hatch by Eileen Spinelli (Simon & Schuster Books for Young Readers, 1996)

Swimmy by Leo Lionni (Dragonfly Books; Reissue Edition, 2017)

The Berenstain Bears and The Joy of Giving by Michael Berenstain and Jan Berenstain (Zonderkidz, 2010)

The Berenstain Bears Think of Those in Need by Stan Berenstain and Jan Berenstain (Random House Books for Young Readers, 1999)

The Carrot Seed, 60th Anniversary Edition by Ruth Krauss (Harper Collins, 2004)

The Family Book by Todd Parr (Little, Brown Books for Young Readers; Reprint Edition, 2010)

The Giving Tree by Shel Silverstein (Harper & Row, 1964)

The Invisible Boy by Trudy Ludwig (Knopf, 2013)

The Librarian of Basra: A True Story from Iraq by Jeanette Winter (Houghton Mifflin Harcourt, 2005)

The Little Red Hen by Paul Galdone (HMH Books for Young Readers; Reprint Edition, 1985)

The Lorax by Dr. Seuss (Random House Books for Young Readers, 1971)

The Mitten by Jan Brett (Putnam Juvenile, 1996)

The Mitten Tree by Candace Christiansen and Elaine Greenstein (Fulcrum Publishing, 2009)

The Name Jar by Yangsook Choi (Dragonfly Books; Reprint Edition, 2003)

The Paper Princess by Elisa Kleven (Puffin Books; Reprint, 1998)

*The Picture Book of Helen Kelle*r by David A. Adler (Holiday House; Reprint Edition, 1990)

The Pirate of Kindergarten by George Ella Lyon (Atheneum/Richard Jackson Books, 2010)

The Quiltmaker's Gift by Jeff Brumbeau and Gail De Marcken (Scholastic Press; 3rd Edition, 2001)

The Sissy Duckling by Harvey Fierstein (Simon & Schuster Books for Young Readers; Reprint Edition, 2005)

The Three Questions by Jon Muth (Scholastic Press, 2002)

The Very Busy Spider by Eric Carle (Philomel Books, 1985)

The Way Back Home by Oliver Jeffers (Philomel Books, 2008)

Two Good Friends by Judy Delton (Crown, 1988)

Wangari's Trees of Peace by Jeanette Winter (Harcourt, 2008)

What Does It Mean To Be Kind? by Rana DiOrio (Little Pickle Press, 2015)

Whoever You Are by Mem Fox (HMH Books for Young Readers, 2006)

Yoko by Rosemary Wells (Disney-Hyperion; Reprint Edition, 2009)

Zen Socks by Jon Muth (Scholastic Press, 2015)

Zen Shorts by Jon Muth (Scholastic Press, 2005)

Zen Ties by Jon Muth (Scholastic Press, 2008)

Books teach children to see
the world through the eyes of others
and empathise with others.
It's about the story.

—*Malorie Blackman, writer*

Recommended Reading for Older Kids

Non-Fiction

77 Creative Ways Kids Can Serve by Sondra Clark (Wesleyan Publishing House, 2008)

Be a Changemaker: How to Start Something That Matters by Laurie Ann Thompson (Simon Pulse/Beyond Words, 2014)

Big Book of Service Projects (Gospel Light, 2001)

Do Something: A Handbook for Young Activists by Nancy Lublin (Workman Publishing, 2010)

Doing Good Together 101 Easy, Meaningful Service Projects for Families, Schools, and Communities by Jenny Friedman and Joelene Roehlkeparpain (Free Spirit Publishing, 2010)

Helping Kids Help by Renee Heiss (Skyhorse Publishing, 2007)

How to Be an Everyday Philanthropist 330 Ways to make a Difference in your Home, Community, and World—At No Cost by Nicole Bouchard Boles (Workman Publishing, 2009)

Hungry Planet: What the World Eats by Peter Menzel and Faith D'Aluisio (Material World Books, 2005)

I Am Malala: How One Girl Stood Up for Education and Changed the World (Young Readers Edition) by Malala Yousafzai (Author), Patricia

McCormick (Contributor) (Little, Brown Books for Young Readers; Reprint Edition, 2016)

Iqbal by Francesco D'Adamo (Alladin; Reprint Edition, 2005)

It's Your World: Get Informed, Get Inspired & Get Going! by Chelsea Clinton (Puffin Books, 2015)

Kids' Random Acts of Kindness (Random Acts of Kindness Series) by Rosalyn Carter (Forward) (Conari Press, 1995)

Kids Who Are Changing the World by Anne Jankeliowitch and Yann Arthus-Bertrand (Sourcebooks Jabberwocky, 2004)

Kids With Courage: True Stories about Young People Making a Difference by Barbara A. Lewis (Free Spirit, 1992)

Malala, a Brave Girl from Pakistan/Iqbal, a Brave Boy from Pakistan: Two Stories of Bravery by Jeanette Winter (Beach Lane Books, 2014)

Olivia's Birds: Saving the Gulf by Olivia Bouler (Sterling, 2011)

Pay It Forward (Young Reader's Edition) by Catherine Ryan Hyde (Simon & Schuster/Paula Wiseman Books, 2014)

Peterson's 150 Ways Teens Can Make a Difference by Marion Salzman and Teresa Reisgies (Peterson Nelnet Co, 1991)

Real Kids, Real Stories, Real Change: Courageous Actions Around the World by Garth Sundem (Free Spirit Publishing, 2010)

Six Million Paper Clips: The Making of a Children's Holocaust Memorial by Peter W. Schroeder and Dagmar Schroeder-Hildebrand (Kar-Ben Publishing 2004)

Teaching Kids to Care and Share: 300+ Mission & Service Ideas for Children by Jolene Roehlkepartain (Abingdon Press, 2002)

The Giving Book by Ellen Sabin (Watering Can, 2004)

The Promise of a Pencil by Adam Braun (Scribner, 2014)

Fiction

Bystander by James Preller (Perfection Learning, 2011)

Fish in a Tree by Lynda Mullaly Hunt (Puffin Books; Reprint Edition, 2017)

Wonder by RJ Palacio (Knopf Books for Young Readers, 2012)

Recommended Reading for Adults:

These are adult books with themes about giving, caring, difference, and compassion that we have enjoyed and found inspiring. We hope they might help you crystallize your thoughts on these topics and, perhaps, offer you a new lens through which to see the world.

A Year of Living Generously: Dispatches from the Front Lines of Philanthropy by Lawrence Scanlan (D&M Adult, 2010)

An Invisible Thread: The True Story of an 11 Year Old Panhandler, a Busy Sales Executive, and an Unlikely Meeting with Destiny by Laura Schroff and Alex Tresniowski (Howard Books, 2011)

Angels on Earth: Inspiring Stories of Fate, Friendship, and The Power of Connections by Laura Schroff and Alex Tresniowski (Simon and Schuster, 2016)

A Path Appears Transforming Lives, Creating Opportunity by Nicholas Kristof and Sheryl WuDunn (Knopf, 2015)

Building Moral Intelligence: The Seven Essential Virtues That Teach Kids to Do the Right Thing by Michele Borba (Jossey Bass, 2002)

E Is for Ethics: How to Talk to Kids about Morals, Values and What Matters Most by Ian James Corlett (Simon and Schuster, 2009)

Everybody's Different by Nancy Miller and Catherine Sammons (Brooks Publishing, 1999)

Giving: How Each of Us Can Change the World by Bill Clinton (Knopf, 2007)

Growing Grateful Kids: Teaching Them to Appreciate an Extraordinary God in Ordinary Places by Susie Larson (Hearts at Home Books, 2010)

Making Grateful Kids; The Science of Building Character by Jeffrey Froh and Giacomo Bono (Templeton Foundation Press, 2014)

Parenting from the Inside Out: How a Deeper Self-Understanding Can Help You Raise Children Who Thrive (10th Anniversary Edition) by Daniel Siegel and Mary Hartzell (Tarcher Perigee, 2013)

Raising Charitable Children by Carol Weisman (F.E. Robbins & Sons Press, 2006)

Raising Happiness: 10 Simple Steps for More Joyful Kids and Happier Parents by Christine Carter (Ballantine Books, 2010)

Raising Respectful Children in a Disrespectful World by Jill Rigby (Howard Books, 2013)

Raising Unselfish Children in a Self-Absorbed World Paperback by Jill Rigby. (Howard Books, 2008).

Rambam's Ladder by Julie Salamon (Workman Publishing, 2003)

Teach Your Children Well by Madeline Levine (HarperCollins, 2013)

Teaching Your Kids to Care: How to Discover and Develop the Spirit of Charity In Your Children by Debbie Spaide (Citadel Press,1995)

The Altruistic Brain: How We are Naturally Good by Ronald Pfaff, PhD with Sandra Sherman (Oxford University Press, 2015)

The Healing Power of Doing Good by Allan Luks with Peggy Payne (iUniverse, 2001)

The Giving Box: Create a Tradition of Giving with Your Children by Fred Rogers (Running Press, 2000)

Soul of a Citizen: Living With Conviction in Challenging Times by Paul Rogath Loeb (St. Martin's Griffin, 2010)

The Gratitude Diaries by Janice Kaplan (Penguin Random House, 2015)

The Me, Me, Me Epidemic: A Step-by-Step Guide to Raising Capable, Grateful Kids in an Over-Entitled World by Amy McCready (TarcherPerigee, 2015)

The Opposite of Spoiled: Raising Kids Who Are Grounded, Generous, and Smart About Money by Ron Lieber (Harper, 2015)

The Power of Giving by Azim Jamal and Harvey McKinnon (TarcherPerigee, 2009)

The Price of Privilege by Madeline Levine (Harper, 2006)

The Road to Character by David Brooks (Random House, 2015)

The Spiritual Child by Lisa Miller (St. Martin's Press, 2015)

The World Needs Your Kid: Raising Children Who Care and Contribute by Craig Kielburger, Marc Kielburger, and Shelley Page (Greystone Books, 2014)

Unselfie: Why Empathetic Kids Succeed in Our All-About-Me World, by Michele Borba (Touchstone, 2016)

Words that Hurt Words that Heal by Joseph Telushkin (William Morrow, 1996)

Apps, Websites, CDs

Here are a few suggestions of other media that we have found useful for relaxation and meditation.

Headspace App: A guided meditation and mindfulness app designed to be used daily by adults and children.

Still Quiet Place CDs for Young Children and Teens, Amy Saltzman, MD: Guided meditation, breathing, and relaxation exercises of varying length available on CD or MP3. An introduction for children, as well as one for adults, is included.

Guided Mindfulness Meditation with John Kabat-Zinn: Jon Kabat-Zinn, PhD, is the founding Executive Director of the Center for Mindfulness in Medicine, Health Care, and Society at the University of Massachusetts Medical School. He is also the founding director of its renowned Stress Reduction Clinic and professor of medicine emeritus at the University of Massachusetts Medical School. He developed this guided mindfulness meditation practice that can be used by adults and older children.

Guided Imagery Scripts by Mellisa Dormoy: Mellisa is the founder of ShambalaKids, as well as a teacher and author with a focus on children's self-esteem and happiness. She has developed and taught many self-improvement programs for both children and adults. http://shambalakids.com.

Journal Pages

In addition to being a place to write your answers to the questions throughout the book, these pages are for taking notes, writing questions, drawing pictures, and keeping track of your ideas and plans. Please use them to your own kindness advantage. Let them be part of the resources that you and your family will keep as you begin the journey that will enhance your lives and the lives of others.

Questions from Chapter 2, Setting a Positive Example

Are those the attitudes you want to pass down to your children or is it time to rethink them?

_____

_____

_____

_____

_____

_____

_____

Think about when you were your child's age. Who do you remember being kind to you? What did they do? How did that make you feel?

_____

_____

_____

_____

_____

_____

_____

When you think about someone kind and compassionate who comes to mind?

_____

_____

_____

_____

_____

_____

What did you observe them do? What did you learn from them? Were there ways you felt you could be like them? As you think about this person now can you describe what makes them seem so kind?

_____

_____

_____

_____

_____

_____

When you were growing up, how did people in your family show that they cared for others?

Think about ways you showed kindness to others when you were a child. What did you do? How did other people respond?

Now that you are a parent, where is kindness demonstrated in your family's everyday life?

Describe ways you notice how other families show caring for others.

_____

_____

_____

_____

_____

_____

_____

Where do you see room for more kindness in your everyday life?

_____

_____

_____

_____

_____

_____

Questionnaire from Chapter 5, Finding "Formal" Experiences

What volunteer experience, if any, did you have as a child?

_____

_____

_____

_____

_____

_____

Was that experience your idea or did someone else initiate it?

_____

_____

_____

_____

_____

_____

Did you go alone or with friends or family?

_____

_____

_____

_____

_____

_____

Was the experience organized through a particular group (religious institution, school)?

_____

_____

_____

_____

_____

_____

_____

Looking back, do you think the experience was age appropriate? Did it reflect your interests?

_____

_____

_____

_____

_____

_____

_____

How did this volunteer experience affect you?

_____

_____

_____

_____

_____

_____

_____

What volunteer experiences did you have as a teenager and have you had as an adult?

_____

_____

_____

_____

_____

_____

_____

If you did volunteer, was it because you cared about a particular cause, because it was the "right" thing to do or because it was what your friends were doing?

_____

_____

_____

_____

_____

_____

If you didn't volunteer, why didn't you?

_____

_____

_____

_____

_____

_____

Are you currently volunteering? Is your volunteer experience satisfying to you? Why or why not?

_____

_____

_____

_____

_____

_____

As a parent interested in bringing volunteerism to your family, think about how your family spends free time.

_____

_____

_____

_____

_____

_____

How much time do you want to commit to a volunteer opportunity?

❏ One time for a few hours
❏ At holidays
❏ Two or three times per year
❏ On a monthly basis
❏ On a weekly basis

What population or topic interests your child and family?

❏ Animals
❏ Children

11

❏ Chronically Ill
❏ Civics
❏ Domestic Violence
❏ Elderly
❏ Environment
❏ Homeless
❏ Hungry
❏ LGBTQ
❏ Mentally Ill
❏ Physically Disabled
❏ Refugees
❏ Veterans
❏ Other _____

What type of setting interests you?

❏ Day Care Program
❏ Hospital
❏ Library
❏ Park
❏ Physical Rehabilitation Facility
❏ Religious Organization
❏ Senior Center
❏ Shelter
❏ Soup Kitchen
❏ Zoo
❏ Other _____

What setting, if any, would you not be comfortable visiting?

_____

_____

_____

_____

_____

_____

_____

Do you have an understanding as to why you are reluctant to go to a particular setting?

_____

_____

_____

_____

_____

What do you want your child to get out of a volunteer experience?

_____

_____

_____

_____

_____

_____

_____

Which of your child's strengths would you like to encourage in a volunteer experience?

_____

_____

_____

_____

_____

_____

Would you prefer a volunteer experience to be just members of your own family?

_____

_____

_____

_____

_____

_____

_____

Would you be open to including another family or your children's friends?

_____

_____

_____

_____

_____

_____

_____

Consider these questions as you and your child research different organizations. We have included space for you to compare two different organizations.

Organization name: _____

What is their mission?

_____
_____
_____
_____

Who runs the organization?

_____
_____
_____

Who or what need do they serve?

_____
_____
_____
_____

How long have they been operating?

_____
_____
_____

Where do they get most of their money from?

_____

_____

_____

_____

How do they spend their money?

_____

_____

_____

_____

How well are they rated by an organization that monitors charities?

_____

_____

_____

_____

How many volunteers do they have?

_____

_____

What do their volunteers typically do?

_____

_____

_____

_____

Organization name: _____

What is their mission?

_____

_____

_____

_____

Who runs the organization?

_____

_____

_____

_____

Who or what need do they serve?

_____

_____

_____

_____

How long have they been operating?

_____

_____

_____

Where do they get most of their money from?

_____

_____

How do they spend their money?

_____

_____

_____

_____

_____

_____

How well are they rated by an organization that monitors charities?

_____

_____

_____

_____

_____

_____

How many volunteers do they have?

_____

_____

What do their volunteers typically do?

_____

_____

_____

_____

_____

_____

End Notes

Introduction

J. Kiley Hamlin, Karen Wynn and Paul Bloom, "Social Evaluation of Preverbal Infants" Nature Volume 450, (2007): Page 557–559.

Chapter 1

1. Ronit Roth-Hanania, Maayan Davidov, Carolyn Zahn-Waxler, "Empathy Development From 8 to 16 Months: Early Signs of Concern for Others" Infant Behavior and Development Volume 34, Issue 3, (2011): Pages 447–458.

2. Psychologists such as Martin Seligman, Daniel Siegel, and Emiliana Simon-Thomas are leaders in this field.

3. Kristin Layous, Hyunjung Lee, Incheol Choi, and Sonja Lyubomirsky, "Culture Matters When Designing a Successful Happiness-Increasing Activity: A Comparison of the United States and South Korea," *Journal of Cross-Cultural Psychology,* 44 (2013): 1294–1303.

4. Kristin Layous, S. Katherine Nelson, Eva Oberle, Kimberley A. Schonert-Reichl, and Sonja Lyubomirsky, "Kindness Counts: Prompting Prosocial Behavior in Preadolescents Boosts Peer Acceptance and Well-being," *PLoS ONE,* 7, e51380 (2012).

5. Lalin Anik, Lara B. Aknin, Michael I. Norton, and Elizabeth W. Dunn. "Feeling Good about Giving: The Benefits (and Costs) of Self-Interested Charitable Behavior." *Harvard Business School Working Paper,* No. 10–012, August 2009.

6. "Allan Luks' Helper's High," 2010. http://allanluks.com/helpers_high.

7. Baraz, James and Alexander, Shoshana. 'The Helper's High,' 2010. https://greatergood.berkeley.edu/article/item/the_helpers_high.

8. Tori DeAngelis, "The Two Faces of Oxytocin: Why Does the 'Tend and Befriend' Hormone Come Into Play At The Best And Worst Of Times?" *Monitor on Psychology* Vol 39, No. 2 (2008): page 30.

9. Tori DeAngelis, "The Two Faces of Oxytocin: Why Does the 'Tend and Befriend' Hormone Come Into Play At The Best And Worst Of Times?" *Monitor on Psychology* Vol 39, No. 2 (2008): page 30.

10. Corporation for National and Community Service, Office of Research and Policy Development. *The Health Benefits of Volunteering: A Review of Recent Research,* Washington, DC 2007. https://www.nationalservice.gov/pdf/07_0506_hbr.pdf

11. Jacoby, Barbara. *Service-Learning in Higher Education: Concepts and Practices.* (San Francisco, C.A.: Jossey-Bass, 1996).

12. Christine I. Celio, Joseph Durlak, Allison Dymnicki, "A Meta-Analysis of the Impact of Service-Learning on Students," *Journal of Experiential Education* Vol 34, Issue 2 (2011): 164–181.

13. DiSalvo, David. Forget Survival Of The Fittest: It is Kindness That Counts. Dacher Keltner Interview by *Scientific American, 2009.*

14. Ronald Pfaff, PhD with Sandra Sherman, *The Altruistic Brain: How We Are Naturally Good* (Oxford University Press, 2015), page 280.

15. J. Kiley Hamlin, Karen Wynn, and Paul Bloom, "3-Month-Olds Show A Negativity Bias In Their Social Evaluations," *Developmental Science* Volume 13, Issue 6 (2010) 923–929.

16. Lara B. Aknin, J. Kiley Hamlin, Elizabeth W. Dunn, "Giving Leads to Happiness in Young Children," *PLoS ONE* Volume 7 Issue 6 (2012): e39211.

17. Doris Bischof-Köhler , "The Development of Empathy in Infants" in *Infant Development: Perspectives from German Speaking Countries,* eds. M. E. Lamb & H. Keller (Hillsdale, NJ:Lawrence Erlbaum, 1991), 245–273.

18. Carolyn Zahn-Waxler, Teach Compassion, filmed in Richmond, C.A. June 2011, TEDx Video. 15:09. https://www.youtube.com/watch?v=sVtXeDcYJfY

19. Joanna Harcourt Smith. 'What Is Innate Kindness?' DharmaPodcast. https://centerhealthyminds.org/join-the-movement/innate-kindness https://centerhealthyminds.org/assets/files-resources/DP802_Richard_Davidson_Innate_Kindness. mp3, *Dharma Podcast at DharmaPodcast.org. This is Upaya Conversations, a monthly podcast series with Joanna Harcourt-Smith. Episode 802 "Innate Kindness."*

20. Carolyn Zahn-Waxler, Teach Compassion, filmed in Richmond, C.A. June 2011, TEDx Video. 15:09. https://www.youtube.com/watch?v=sVtXeDcYJfY

Chapter 2:

1. Keiko Otake, Satoshi Shimai, Junko Tanaka-Matsumi, Kanako Otsui, & Barbara L. Fredrickson, "Happy People Become Happier Through Kindness: A Counting Kindnesses Intervention," *Journal of Happiness Studies,* Volume 7 (2006): 361–375.

Chapter 4:

1. Lewis, Dyani. "UpClose" Podcast. *Where's Your Compassion? Generation Y and the New Empathy Deficit, 2013.* https://upclose.unimelb.edu.au/episode/246-where-s -your-compassion-generation-y-and-new-empathy-deficit#transcription.

Chapter 5:

1. S. Katherine Nelson, Matthew D. Della Porta, Katherine Jacobs Bao, HyunJung Crystal Lee, Incheol Choi & Sonja Lyubomirsky (2014): 'It's up to you': Experimentally manipulated autonomy support for prosocial behavior improves well-being in two cultures over six weeks, *The Journal of Positive Psychology: Dedicated to furthering research and promoting good practice,* DOI: 10.1080/17439760.2014.983959.

2. Weinstein, N., & Ryan, R. M. (2010). "When Helping Helps: Autonomous Motivation for prosocial behavior and its influence on well-being for the helper and recipient." *Journal of Personality and Social Psychology,* 98, 222–244.

3. Doris Bischof-Köhler, "The Development of Empathy in Infants," *In Infant Development: Perspectives from German Speaking Countries,* ed. M. E. Lamb & H. Keller (Hillsdale, NJ: Lawrence Erlbaum, 1991) 245–273.

4. Laura Littlepage, Elizabeth Obergfell, Gina Zanin (2003). *Family Volunteering: An Exploratory Study of the Impact on Families.* Indianapolis: Indiana University–Purdue University Indianapolis, School of Public and Environmental Affairs, Center for Urban Policy and the Environment.

5. Laura Littlepage, Elizabeth Obergfell, Gina Zanin (2003). *Family Volunteering: An Exploratory Study of the Impact on Families.* Indianapolis: Indiana University–Purdue University Indianapolis, School of Public and Environmental Affairs, Center for Urban Policy and the Environment.

Chapter 6:

1. Dr. Maria Napoli, Paul Rock Krech & Lynn C. Holley (2008) Mindfulness Training for Elementary School Students, Journal of Applied School Psychology, 21:1, 99–125, DOI: 10.1300/J370v21n01_05

2. A.S.,Koeppen, "Relaxation Training For Children." *Elementary School Guidance and Counseling,* 9, (1974); 14–21.

3. Sandi Shwartz, "How to Teach Children Loving Kindness Meditation." Sharon Salzberg (blog), February 25, 2016. https://www.sharonsalzberg.com/teach-children-loving kindness-meditation/.

4. Lauren Chaitoff, "Loving-Kindness Meditation for Kids and Valentines." *YogaDork* (blog), 2015 http://yogadork.com/2015/02/11/loving-kindness-meditation-for -kids-and-valentines/.

Acknowledgments

Dale and Amanda wish to acknowledge:

We have received so many kindnesses from people since we began this journey that acknowledging everyone is nearly impossible. There are, however, a handful of people whose enthusiasm and help made it possible for us to complete this book. Thank you to:

Pam Bernstein and Jonathan Kolatch who offered their encouragement, guidance, and direction in the earliest stages.

The many friends, relatives, colleagues, and clergy who took the time to share their thoughts about charity and giving with us. Specifically: Rabbi Sheldon Zimmerman, Rabbi Hanniel Levinson, Rabbi Mitchell Hurvitz, Rabbi Sherre Hirsch, Reverend Susan Sparks, Reverend Heather Wright, Divya Sareen, Miriam Sumner, Willy Sumner, Janet Weathers, Warren Estabrooks, Carolee Lee, Maggie Kneip, Ken Levinson, Jim Grissom, Janet Slom, Helen Sachs Chaset, Pam Ehrenkranz, Yumi Mera Kuwana, David Waren, Claire Ciliotta, and Norma Feshbach.

Julie Mazur Tribe who shared her positive spirit along with sharp editorial skills and experience as a mother of a young child.

Marcia Ciriello and T. Cooper who made us look and feel terrific.

Karen Gantz, agent extraordinaire, who believed in the importance of our message and worked tirelessly on our behalf.

And, of course, the team at HCI where our book found its home who encouraged us: our editor, Allison Janse along with Ian Briggs and Kim Weiss.

Dale wishes to acknowledge:

Amanda. You are wise, patient, and focused. My love, respect, and admiration for you is immeasurable. This journey took more time than expected but exactly as much time as needed. I am grateful to you for going the distance.

Rob Rosen: You are my heart. Your love gives me strength every day. I appreciate the way you notice what is needed in our family, with our friends, and in the wider community. You notice and then you "show up" to be of service. And, you fill me with love and laughter.

My parents: Jerry (of blessed memory) and Sylvia Atkins. You raised my sister, Daryl, and me to be appreciative of our lives while being mindful of the lives of others. Your message was no act of kindness is too small and do whatever we can to help improve the world. Daryl and Steven Roth: both generous and giving. You raised Amanda and Jordan to be caring, decent, charitable adults. With you as their parental role models, each, with their loving spouses, Michael and Richie, is changing the world in profound ways.

Jono, Josh, Tracy, and Yael: You are the source of my deep joy and with all that you have on your very full plates, your thoughtfulness is ever present. I admire the way you are raising your children to be engaged in the world for good. Ross, Maya, Eitan, Eli, Asher and Ayla: My love for you is bigger than the number of stars in the sky and the grains of sand on the seashore.

I am blessed and grateful for my family, friends, clients, and colleagues who have shown me countless acts of kindness and appreciation throughout my life. Janet W., Laurie W., Helen C., Janet S., Rona J., Ruth H., Nelly B., Ji-Eun W., Nan L., Carolee L., Maggie K., Gary S., Linda A., Yumi K., Jane B., Ahuva S., Nancy H., Susan R., Adria R., Kusum G., Carina C., Brooke S., Madhu M., Claire C., Jeannemarie B., Kate N., Dawn J., Claire R., Fatima H., Kristine H., Eileen B., Annie G., Sharon E., and the Bookies. Thank you all for being there in your very YOU-nique ways.

Amanda wishes to acknowledge:

Dale. Thank you for asking me to join you on what has been quite an adventure! I'm grateful that we made it to the finish line together.

So many friends, colleagues, and relatives have shared their enthusiasm for this book and its message throughout the process. Thank you. There are a few, however, who deserve special mention. Allison Rosier, Beth Zuriff, and Ellen Lowey forever my B's; all things books begin and end with you. Beth Kobliner and Elisa Port. You are both examples of caring moms, the kindest friends, and busy professionals who made writing books look easy. Thank you for providing much needed motivation and inspiration. Riverdale Yogis. Tuesdays and Thursdays have become days to share friendship, calm, and tales of marriage and parenting. Thank you. Devorah Nazarian, Page Bondor, and Evie Klein have, for many years, been among my dearest "mommy friends." Thanks to each of you for sharing the most joyful and most challenging parenting moments.

Daryl and Steven Roth, my favorite parents. Thank you for being such good role models in this arena. And, of course, for always being my biggest supporters. Love you both. Jordan Roth, dearest brother, if only I had your PR savvy this book would already be a best-seller. Michael Salzhauer, you are my love and partner in crime. Rebecca, Abigail, and Emily, you are each your own strong, smart, wonderful young woman. You fill my life with laughter, perpetual motion, and tremendous pride. I love you more than you can imagine.